LET YOUR DREAMS
BE YOUR DOCTOR

LET YOUR DREAMS
BE YOUR DOCTOR

Using Dreams to Diagnose and Treat Physical and Emotional Problems

ARLENE SHOVALD PH.D.

BALBOA PRESS
A DIVISION OF HAY HOUSE

Copyright © 2011 Arlene Shovald Ph.D.

All rights reserved. No part of this book may be used or reproduced by any means, graphic, electronic, or mechanical, including photocopying, recording, taping or by any information storage retrieval system without the written permission of the publisher except in the case of brief quotations embodied in critical articles and reviews.

Balboa Press books may be ordered through booksellers or by contacting:

Balboa Press
A Division of Hay House
1663 Liberty Drive
Bloomington, IN 47403
www.balboapress.com
1-(877) 407-4847

Because of the dynamic nature of the Internet, any web addresses or links contained in this book may have changed since publication and may no longer be valid. The views expressed in this work are solely those of the author and do not necessarily reflect the views of the publisher, and the publisher hereby disclaims any responsibility for them.

The author of this book does not dispense medical advice or prescribe the use of any technique as a form of treatment for physical, emotional, or medical problems without the advice of a physician, either directly or indirectly. The intent of the author is only to offer information of a general nature to help you in your quest for emotional and spiritual well-being. In the event you use any of the information in this book for yourself, which is your constitutional right, the author and the publisher assume no responsibility for your actions.

Any people depicted in stock imagery provided by Thinkstock are models, and such images are being used for illustrative purposes only.
Certain stock imagery © Thinkstock.

ISBN: 978-1-4525-3483-1 (e)
ISBN: 978-1-4525-3482-4 (sc)
ISBN: 978-1-4525-3484-8 (hc)

Library of Congress Control Number: 2011907530

Printed in the United States of America

Balboa Press rev. date: 6/1/2011

ACKNOWLEDGEMENTS

A book like this is never the work of just one person. It is a compilation of contributions from people who have contributed to the study of dreams throughout history. In this case, the work goes back as far as Hippocrates, the Father of Medicine, who recognized the value of dreams in diagnosis and treatment of physical and emotional problems that modern day physicians have only recently begun to acknowledge.

I thank the many teachers who worked with me during the time I was writing my doctoral dissertation on dream work. This includes not only those who served as formal instructors but also those who contributed in informal ways through sharing thoughts and information about their own dreams.

Thanks especially to the 14 individuals who will remain anonymous who so kindly shared their dreams for this study. Their trust and interest was phenomenal. Without their dream reports this study would not have been possible.

Thank you to G. William Domhoff, Professor of Psychology and Sociology at the University of California – Santa Cruz for sharing valuable information on his methods of dream analysis, and to Stephen Atwood, Ph.D. for serving as my advisor and consultant through the time I was working on the dissertation which ultimately became "Let Your Dreams Be Your Doctor."

Thanks to Curtis Killorn for doing the artwork which I am totally incapable of doing and finally thanks to Pat Windolph, former editor of The Mountain Mail newspaper, for editing the first draft and to author, Armando Benetiz, for editorial suggestions and additions which contributed to the completed product.

FOREWORD

Historically dreams have run the gamut from being accepted as cryptic messages from guardian entities, warning or advising the dreamer of things to come, to meaningless nonsense, as taught by the Christian church in later centuries.

But many of us have always known there are hidden messages in our dreams. "Let Your Dreams Be Your Doctor" is another of many books that provides us with evidence that there is a wealth of information to be found in our dreams.

We may never understand the source of those messages, but whenever we experience a vivid and puzzling dream we are left with a feeling that we should pay attention. We may not have been sure what the symbols meant but there was that "gut feeling" author Arlene Shovald alludes to several times, that tells us something about that dream was important.

"Let Your Dreams Be Your Doctor," teaches the dreamer how to get the most out of the information that is passed down during the night through the veil that separates the unconscious from the conscious.

While dream dictionaries are helpful in deciphering the dream code, they are just one part of the solution to the puzzle. As the author explains, dreams are unique to the individual; so two people having virtually the same dream will find a different meaning in it.

The information in this book will guide the reader in translating the message of their dreams into understandable information. Dr. Shovald contrasts her own approach of using dreams to diagnose physical ailments to the view supported by Armando Benitez (*Sheer*

Superstition), who tells us that our precognitive dreams are the result of our subconscious incursions into the realms of the arcane.

The fact that the author has relied on dreams for information regarding her physical and emotional health for many years is impressive in itself, but she has taken it a step further and broadened the study to include the dreams of 14 other individuals, male and female, ranging in age from 8 to 81, in various stages of emotional and physical health ranging from those with no indications of imbalance to those nearing the end of their lives.

Doctoral dissertations, with their heavy academic language and boring statistics, make for dull reading, but the author has taken the time to "translate" her doctoral dissertation on "Using Dreams to Diagnose and Treat Physical and Emotional Problems" into a "reader friendly" and informative piece of literature that provides a starting point for the novice to dream interpretation and a fresh, new view on the subject to seasoned dream journalists.

Consider this an important addition to your library of metaphysical and spiritual studies.

Henry Hollenbaugh
(Author of *Rio San Pedro*)

INTRODUCTION

As I was nearing the end of 10 years of study toward a doctorate in Transpersonal Psychology in January 1998, I was faced with deciding on a topic for my dissertation. With a focus on mind/body/spirit healing and an emphasis on hypnotherapy and past life regression therapy, there were several topics that interested me, but for some reason, working with dreams, specifically to diagnose and treat physical and emotional problems, kept coming up.

It wasn't just that the study of dreams had always fascinated me. It went deeper than that. Partly, I think it went all the way back to childhood when I often had dreams that "came true." One, in particular, was about my Uncle What. Ainer was Finnish, as were many of the people in Iron River in Michigan's Upper Peninsula, where I grew up. He also worked in the woods, one of the primary occupations there.

I don't remember how old I was, but I'm guessing I was about 12 when I dreamed Ainer was walking in the woods, holding the hands of his two little daughters, one on each side. The scene in the woods was beautiful. It was sunny and bright and not at all formidable and they were walking down a path when suddenly a bluebird came down and landed on my uncle's neck and the dream stopped. It was like the film suddenly snapped in a movie.

I didn't think any more about it until later that day when my mother got a phone call saying Uncle Ainer had been killed. He was working in the woods when he was struck by a "widow maker" – a branch that got hung up in a tree and suddenly let loose, came crashing down on him, breaking his neck.

I remember getting a silly grin on my face, not knowing how to respond, because what had happened to my uncle was almost identical to what I had seen happen to him in my dream. I'll never forget that awkward feeling, not knowing whether I should laugh or cry and wanting to tell someone about the dream, but at the same time knowing it wasn't something I should talk about. I grew up Catholic in a very conservative community, where anything that bordered on the occult was just not "right" and, aside from the ghost stories of the "olden days" that my Irish grandmother told once in awhile for fun, such things as dream predictions, fortune telling and ghosts were simply not taken seriously. After all, that was a "sin." The Church said so.

Another precognitive dream occurred before my Aunt Ina died. I only met her once or twice, but after she departed from one of those brief visits, I had a dream that she was eaten alive by spiders. Not long after, my parents received a call that Ina had cancer. Before long, she was dead. Again, I never said a word, but it certainly got me to thinking about dreams and where they come from and, even at that young age, I realized there was more to them than just aimless ramblings that took up time during the night.

About the same time, probably when I was middle school age, I began to utilize my dreams as plots for short stories. I was probably one of a handful of people who actually welcomed nightmares. They made great stories for horror comics. I never sold any of them, but they got me started in my career as a writer.

I guess I should mention also that while I was at that point of deciding on a dissertation topic, I was not your average "college kid." I was 58 years old.

Writing was my first career and, through the years, while our four children were growing up, I had written pretty much anything (freelance) that the magazines would buy. I also wrote a column for our local newspaper, The Reporter, called "Around the House With Arlene." It was rather like Erma Bombeck, although I had not heard of her at the time, and readers seemed to enjoy it.

When the editor left, I was offered his position. By then the kids were all in school, so without benefit of a degree in journalism I became the editor of The Reporter, a weekly newspaper with a circulation of about 5,000.

I suffered from allergies all my life and they turned into severe asthma, which resulted in a Near Death Experience on March 15, 1978. I didn't know anything about Near Death Experiences (NDE's) at the time but the last thing I remember was struggling for air in my hospital bed and then my grandma, who had been dead about 10 years, was sitting at the foot of my bed with her hair wound up in the little bun she always wore, and wearing her apron. My husband was also standing beside me and it never occurred to me as being strange that grandma and my husband were both "solid" figures with one as real as the other.

I felt myself floating up out of the bed, following Grandma down what appeared to be a glass tunnel. I even remember looking down on the grass in the field next to the hospital and noticing the ice crystals on the blades of grass. Everything was very sharp and clear.

The other strange thing was that Grandma and I were communicating telepathically – not with spoken words. But of course at the time that also seemed perfectly normal.

There was a very bright light at the end of the tunnel and when we got to what seemed to be halfway there, I told Grandma I had to go back. There were things I had to do. She said it was okay if I felt I had something to finish up.

Suddenly I felt like I was slammed back into my hospital bed. I remember feeling like I had actually bounced on the mattress, as though I had fallen from a height. When I woke up my breathing was back to normal the people around me were crying and my first thought was someone I knew had died, because I knew all the hospital people from working on the local ambulance.

When I told them about my experience I was assured that people often "hallucinate" like that when they are low on oxygen and/or on medication, and I bought that theory until many years later when I learned NDE's were, in fact, quite common and my experience was nearly a textbook version of what one was like.

After that NDE, I was sent to National Jewish Hospital in Denver, Colorado with the grim prediction that I had only six months to live if I didn't get to a warmer, drier climate. By then our two oldest children were out of school, so my husband and I and the two youngest moved to Salida, Colorado, a small town in the Rocky Mountains with a population of about 5,000. Initially, there were no jobs open at the newspaper and because I had background as an Emergency Medical Technician, I took a job at the local hospital as a nurse's aide. After 18 months, an opening came up for a reporter at The Mountain Mail newspaper and I went back to my first love – writing.

All of this time I was still doing freelance writing. Because of my severe asthma and serious reactions to so many medications that I took for it, I had accumulated a lot of knowledge about mind/body/spirit healing but was unable to get anything on the subject of health published. Several times, publishers said an article was "interesting" but because I had no credentials (being an EMT didn't count) they couldn't use it. So at age 49 I decided to get some credentials and spent the next 10 years going to college part-time and working at the newspaper fulltime to get letters after my name to qualify me to write about the things I already knew about.

It didn't make a lot of sense, but I must admit I enjoyed almost every minute of it. (Except for algebra and statistics!)

I was nearly finished with my Ph.D. in Transpersonal Psychology, literally down to the wire and starting the dissertation, when everything came to a screaming halt in March 1998. I had decided the topic of my dissertation would be "Using Dreams To Diagnose and Treat Physical and Emotional Problems."

Then I got pneumonia. I was told I had to have an antibiotic. Having taken several antibiotics over the years and experienced bad reactions to all of them, I was very much afraid, but my doctor assured me he had a new one, a fluoroquinolone antibiotic, and it would be safe.

What I did not know at the time is that many of the antibiotics in the fluoroquinolone group had caused life threatening and life changing reactions in the people who took them.

I was one of the unlucky ones and spent the next two years barely able to function. The antibiotic apparently did brain chemistry damage and caused a whole lot of problems that make me cringe even as I write about them. But that is a whole "nother" story I won't get into it here, except to say if you are interested in more information, read "Bitter Pills – Inside the Hazardous World of Legal Drugs" by Stephen Fried. Fried's wife, Diane, also a writer, suffered reactions very similar to mine.

I prayed to die. My prayers weren't answered. But about a year into this nightmare I had a dream, which convinced me of the worthiness of my dissertation project on dreams.

I love Halloween and pumpkins, and in the dream I was in a pumpkin patch. The patch was on a steep hillside and it was dry and dusty and the pumpkins and vines were all withered and dying. I managed to crawl up the hill, clawing in the dirt and grasping the dying vines as I made my way to the top. When I finally got there and could see the other side, there were thousands of big, beautiful orange pumpkins, as far as the eye could see. It was like an ocean of pumpkins under a beautiful blue sky! The vines were healthy and green and suddenly I knew I was going to recover. I had no idea how long it would take but I knew it would happen.

It took two years, but eventually I regained my ability to sleep, the 24/7 nausea subsided, the anxiety and panic attacks began to go away and it became apparent I was going to be able to go on with my life. Once again, a dream had come true. A dream had become my doctor, giving me the inspiration to continue when it seemed I was never again going to lead a normal life.

It is my hope that this book will enable you to allow your dreams to be your doctor, and of course, it goes without saying that if your dreams indicate you should see your doctor, by all means listen!

CHAPTER ONE

Doctors Who Don't Speak Your Language

Have you ever gone to a doctor – perhaps a very good doctor – who was from another country and spoke another language? You probably found it difficult to understand what he/she was saying and were frustrated because you knew this doctor had some good information, if only you could figure out what he/she was trying to say.

Possibly you may have had the same problem with doctors who used confusing medical terms you didn't understand and didn't have the time to explain them to you in "English." Maybe you even had to go home and look up the words to figure out your problem.

Dreams are a lot like that. When you use your dreams to guide you in diagnosing and treating your own physical and emotional problems, it's like having a doctor who speaks a foreign language. Your dreams have valuable information, specifically about you, but you have to figure out what they're trying to tell you. That takes time and patience and a willingness to figure out the symbolic language of your dreams. But as someone who has used dreams for years as a means of health advisory, I can tell you, it's worth the effort.

At first "Dr. Dream" seems to be speaking in a foreign language, causing you to scratch your head and wonder what on earth dead plants, for example, have to do with that tired feeling you've been having, or what a dream about a filthy kitchen could possibly have to do with your health, especially since your own kitchen is neat and tidy and bears no resemblance to the messy one in your dreams. And what about that messy attic – when you live in an apartment or don't even have an attic?

The key to understanding the information dreams provide through your higher self lies in symbology. Just as you sometimes need a medical dictionary to figure out what that report from your doctor means, a good book on dream symbols is a must if you want to decipher the symbols in your dreams.

There are plenty of good dream dictionaries on the market, which is why I've opted not to include one in this book, other than the mention of some basic symbols which are pretty much universal. Having spent hundreds of dollars on dream books and dream dictionaries, the three I would recommend most, in this order, are "The Dream Book – Symbols For Self Understanding" by Betty Bethards (ISBN 1-86204-098-2, Element Books, Inc. 1995); "The Mystical Magical Marvelous World of Dreams" by Wilda B. Tanner (ISBN 0 - 945027-02-8, Sparrow Hawk Press) and "The Bedside Dream Dictionary" by Silvana Amar (ISBN 978-1-60239-1-138-3, Skyhorse Publishing, Inc.) All three are inexpensive, yet include a comprehensive list of dream symbols that will help you decipher the information your dreams reveal to you.

Sometimes your specific symbol may not be listed but rest assured (no pun intended), that's okay. As you progress with your study of dreams and their meanings you will learn that meanings of symbols are specific to the individual. A snake, for example, may be terrifying to one person and a symbol of hope to another. If you have always been afraid of snakes and encounter one in your dreams, chances are there is something going on in your life you are afraid of. On the other hand, if you associate the snake with the shedding of its skin (shedding old, outdated concepts) and growing a fresh new skin, then a dream of a snake would have an entirely different meaning. For me, a snake is a symbol of healing as represented by the two serpents entwined around a staff on the medical symbol, the caduceus

Our subconscious has a way of figuring it all out, sending us symbols which are unique and meaningful to the individual. Two people can have basically the same dream but that dream will have different meanings, depending on the race, gender, religion, education, and life experience of the individual.

Dream dictionaries are a good guide, especially when a person is just beginning to pay attention to dreams and trying to figure them out, but they aren't the total answer, as you discover when you delve into this magical and meaningful world of nocturnal entertainment and information.

Not all dreams, however, are symbolic. Some deliver information that is straight to the point and require no decoding. I call these informative dreams. Sometimes they come in the form of a message from a deceased loved one. Personally, I think it may actually be a message from the loved one, but the explanation, if you don't believe in spirits or a life after death, is that our subconscious provides us with information we need by "sending it" in a way that we will most likely accept it. So it may not be the spirit of your deceased Aunt Sara warning you to check the brakes on your car, but it may very well be your subconscious sending you that information in a way you will accept – from Aunt Sara. Assuming you loved and trusted her and valued what she had to say, you are much more likely to heed a warning from her than if it came from your fourth grade school teacher who pulled the hair on the back of your neck to get your attention.

Precognitive dreams are yet another category. We all know of situations when someone had a dream and then it (or something very similar) happened. My dream about my uncle, the logger, was one of those. There was some symbology in that dream as well, but more prominent was the message of something about to happen. However, even had I known then, as a child, what I know now about dreams, I am quite sure no one would have paid any attention had I warned them. Unfortunately, the meaning of precognitive dreams is seldom "clear" initially. Also, Western culture and religions do not usually value the information in dreams. People, in general, seldom heed warnings delivered through dreams or even take time to figure them out, so I am confident there was nothing I could have done to avert that tragedy.

People have dreamed of personal events as well as events in the community, in the nation, and even on the other side of the world, only to discover later on that they actually happened. Sometimes they have even tried to warn those who might be affected, but are they taken seriously? Not usually. So the purpose of this book is certainly not to help you become a prophet, but rather, to provide a guide to help you recognize dreams that indicate pending problems so you can "head them off at the pass" – so to speak. Fortunately, as I write this, Western society is now becoming more attuned to the value of dreams. TV programs like "Medium," for example, are calling attention to real people who use their dreams in everyday life with meaningful results. What was once considered "far out" and "imagination" is gradually becoming accepted and I have no doubt that in the future, medical doctors, like alternative healers, will pay close attention when patients reveal a message that came to them in a dream. In fact, some already do! But most of them aren't likely to admit it just yet.

We like to pride ourselves on living in a modern society where nothing is accepted as fact unless it is scientifically provable through diagnostic tests, double blind studies or other accepted documentation, so we are often reluctant to even admit information came through a dream or intuition or anything other than rock solid, provable hard facts. As a result, we are the losers.

Native Americans and other tribal cultures, historically, have relied on dreams to guide them in their daily lives. I have a dear friend who is a Lakota Sioux and to this day her people work with dreams to find answers to problems in their lives.

"If we have a vibrant dream we go to the medicine man and gift him with tobacco and ask his help," she told me. " Sometimes he meditates and prays over it first and is answered by the spirits. We can also give our dreams to a wise woman or elder. Usually dreams are held in confidence, like confessions made to a priest. Dreams tell us of our abilities. As an example, a dream might tell us we have the ability to become a healer or a war chief., but part of the rule is you can't tell anyone else your dream; only the medicine man or elder."

To help facilitate the dream and keep the memory intact, the Lakota often put something to remind them of the dream in a medicine bag. A feather, for example, to remind them of an eagle, or a stone to remind them of a mountain. This is a practice that could easily be applied by the rest of us. Make or buy a little medicine bag and put symbols of the dreams you want to remember in it. Even a small plastic baggie will work and it can be easily carried in your purse or pants pocket.

The Senoi in Malaysia are perhaps the best example of a culture that actually relies on dreams to guide them. Every morning family members review their dreams of the night before and unlike our "modern" cultures, where children are often criticized for having an overactive imagination, Senoi children are praised for reporting their dreams, which are shared with other members of the tribe if it seems pertinent.

The Senoi use dreams to solve everyday problems and life situations. Victimization is a frequent factor in dreams, not just with the Senoi, but also for people in general. The difference is, the Senoi deal with victimization in dreams by confronting and conquering the images. Patricia Garfield, Ph.D., in "Creative Dreaming" (Ballantine Books, 1985) tells how Senoi parents begin working with their children, listening to their dreams, as soon as they are able to talk. The children are taught how to react to dream situations and characters and by the time they are adolescents, they no longer have nightmares and are using their dreams creatively to benefit themselves, their family and their tribe. The Senoi are also a peaceful culture. Violence is rare. This is certainly not something we can say about our "civilized" culture. So I ask, who is the more civilized? And is it possible the Senoi work out their aggressions in the dream state and thus devote their time in the waking state to more productive endeavors?

Most dreams have messages to impart. However, some dreams just reprocess the day's events. This type of dream is sometimes referred to as a "day residue" dream. We relive the events of the day in our sleep. And, of course, there could still be a solution to a problem in this type of dream. We've all heard the expression "sleep on it" to get an answer. And it's true. Sometimes answers really do come that way. Probably the best example is the invention of the sewing machine. Elias Howe had been trying to figure out how to make a machine that would sew, but nothing worked. One day he gave up, took a nap and had a nightmare in which he was being chased by a group of savage warriors. The strange thing was their spears had holes in the tips! Upon awaking he thought about the dream and was inspired to put the hole in the needle at the tip rather than at the top, and voila! The sewing machine.

Whether he programmed his dreams for an answer or his subconscious just provided him with it, we don't know. What we do know is we can thank a dream for making it possible for us to have mass manufactured clothing rather than being dependent on seamstresses.

Probably the only "meaningless" type of dream I can think of is the dream where you have done something repetitious all day long and then find yourself doing the same thing all night. I had one of those dreams back in the 1960s and I remember it well. I visited a local strawberry patch and picked berries all day, only to return home that evening, dead tired, still faced with the chore of cleaning the berries before I could put them in the refrigerator until the next day when I was going to make jam. That night it was no surprise when I found myself literally seeing red all night long in my dreams as I picked strawberries from dark to dawn in my sleep. That was when I realized the fallacy that was prevalent at that time - that all dreams are in black and white. This certainly was in color and plenty of it. And it didn't mean a thing except that I was tired of picking strawberries and probably not looking forward to making jam with them the next day.

Past life dreams are another type. These dreams provide us with a glimpse into a past we don't consciously remember but the memories are retained in our cells, possibly inherited memories from ancestors. Past life dreams will usually feature characters in old-fashioned clothing or be set in old-fashioned towns or cities and usually everything will be consistent with that time period. You probably won't, for example, find yourself driving up the street in a modern SUV in one of these dreams. You'll be in a horse and carriage or a Model A or whatever the transportation of that time happened to be.

Past life dreams can be therapeutic because they shed light on present day problems, including physical and emotional difficulties that plague us today.

Armando Benitez, author of "Sheer Superstition – Outmaneuvering Fate," (Hampton Roads Publishing, 2000) doesn't believe in past lives. He believes, instead, in multiple realities. Life, he says, involves a constant migration from one reality to another, and sometimes we carry memories from one of these realities to another. But for myself, "past lives" is the more believable and practical explanation for confused memories.

Another consideration with regard to "past lives" is that the memory may be genetic – that is, passed down through the generations and originating not with the dreamer but with an ancestor of the dreamer. The important thing to remember with a dream that appears to be from a past life is that the content of the dream can always be helpful to the dreamer. Whether it is truly a "past life" isn't that important. In working with hypnotherapy clients on "past life" issues, I also stress this. Whether you "believe in" past lives or not isn't important. Whatever comes up is unique to you so you can work with it. Call it imagination if you will, but it is YOUR imagination.

So how do we know what kind of dream we're having and what the message is? The answer, in a nutshell, is "gut feeling." Pay attention to your own intuition. Once you begin working with dreams, writing them down and taking the time to decipher them, you'll understand what I mean. Again, there is nothing "scientific" about it. Your "gut feeling" will let you know if you are interpreting the symbols correctly and what the dream is trying to tell you and once you figure it out, that "aha" feeling will assure you you're "right on."

Read on…

CHAPTER TWO

A Hairy Butt

You already have the answers to your questions in your subconscious and/or higher conscious mind, and you can tap into this vast store of wisdom whenever you need it by learning to decode the language of your dreams.

Dreams can:
- Alert you to physical and emotional health problems before they manifest on a physical level;
- Provide answers to questions;
- Inspire creativity.

Writers are always advised to write about what they know, which is one of the reasons I chose to write about "Using Dreams to Diagnose and Treat Physical and Emotional Problems" for my doctoral dissertation in Transpersonal Psychology.

Dreams have always been an important part in my life, whether they were precognitive dreams, dreams that inspired creative writing or dreams that offered a solution to a problem.

My "hairy butt" dream was one of the latter and a funny one at that, if my problem hadn't been so serious. In March 1997 I was sitting on a chair in my office when suddenly it slipped out from under me, sending me crashing onto the brick floor on my butt. Admittedly, I had plenty of "padding," which should have helped, but I guess it wasn't enough because three nights later I woke up in the middle of the night barely able to move. The next day a visit to the chiropractor helped but it wasn't the total answer. Sciatica tends to recur in some people and I was one of them. I'd just think I had it "fixed" and it would strike again with a vengeance. This went on for several months and I was beginning to think it would never get any better. Then one night while suffering a particularly painful bout, I programmed my dreams for an answer. Prior to going to sleep, I told myself I would have a dream that would tell me what to do about the sciatica.

That night I dreamed of a naked person, seen from behind, with hair on the lower part of the right buttock! I was never sure if the figure was male or female, which could be significant in some situations, but in this case it didn't matter.

A male figure usually represents a conscious aspect of yourself. A female indicates a subconscious or unconscious (and usually nurturing) aspect of yourself – something you haven't quite recognized about yourself on a conscious level.

The dream was so funny and seemed to make no sense at all! Why on earth was I dreaming about a hairy butt when I wanted to know what to do to stop the pain of sciatica? I decided it made no sense. I'd have to try again for an answer. But three days later, when the sciatica was especially painful, it occurred to me that if I elevated my right leg "just a hair" it might help.

Suddenly I realized the significance of the hairy buttocks and found myself laughing in spite of the pain. The pain of sciatica extends down the spinal column and buttocks and radiates down one or both legs, sometimes all the way to the foot, which mine was doing. The figure in my dream had hair growing on the buttocks, right where the sciatic nerve is located and it was on the right side of the body – the side that was affected.

I bought a lift for my shoe and elevated the right leg "just a hair" and experienced some reduction of pain. It was as though I'd been given a prescription from the subconscious.

Later, I learned another secret of programming dreams, which has since been very helpful when asking for information. When issuing an order for a dream to solve a problem, be as specific as possible and present it in a seven-syllable comment. I wish I could remember the origin of the seven-syllable information, but unfortunately I don't. However, I have heard it on several occasions and it appears the reason for the seven-syllable command is that is what the "Western" mind most readily accepts. For those from Eastern cultures, nine syllables are permissible.

Focusing on a problem you could use the generic, seven syllable command – a dream will bring the answer. But the more specific the better. A better command for my sciatica problem, for example, may have been –

- Sci-a-ti-ca go a-way, or,
- My sci-a-ti-ca is gone.

Repeat the command at least three times before going to sleep.

Not long after having my "hairy butt" dream, I happened to come upon some information that ultimately solved my sciatica problem altogether, and this again, is common when working with dreams. I discovered a homeopathic drop called Sciatica, made by Natures Sunshine Products. I haven't had the problem since, and it has now been several years.

In working with dreams you program your subconscious to provide you with the answers you need and as a result you become more aware of information coming your way from other sources. It's very much like hypnotherapy in which you are given a suggestion in the trance state and then put it into action in your "waking" life. You are more tuned in to whatever information comes your way about your problem. It may seem like an accident, but it never is. You may "just happen" to overhear a conversation in a restaurant, you hear an advertisement on the radio or a friend tells you about a great doctor who helped her with the same problem you have.

Of course, if the dream doesn't make any sense (like the hairy butt) it's not much help. This is where a good dream dictionary, like the ones mentioned earlier, comes in. If the dream dictionary doesn't list exactly what you're looking for, it can still be useful. Just look up something that closely resembles your symbol. For example, if a coffee table is a prominent feature in your dream, you may not find coffee table in a dream dictionary, but you more than likely will find table. A table generally represents eating or "tabling a decision" – putting something off.

Now think about a coffee table and how it is different and how it is the same as a regular table. It has shorter legs (are your legs shorter than someone you are competing with in a race?) It may be in the center of the room. (Do you want to be the center of attention?) It may hold books with photographs or information (are you looking for an answer?) or the daily newspaper (is something currently going on in your town or in your life that is bothering you?) Don't be afraid to use your imagination. Contrary to what you were probably taught back in grade school, imagination is not a "four letter word." Imagination is a good thing.

Your dream coffee table may be a mess with food stains and crumbs and ashtrays, or it may be immaculate, with only an expensive "coffee table book" on top. Whichever the case, ask yourself how that coffee table relates to your life. Get creative. Let the thoughts flow and write them down without mentally editing them out of your mind. When you hit upon the "right" meaning, you'll know. You'll get that "aha" feeling we recognize when we realize the answer.

What I call my "balloon method" of analyzing dream symbols is helpful in a case like this. The "balloon method" seemed to be a logical thing to call it since I write the symbol I'm trying to define inside a circle that looks like a balloon. Then I draw lines coming out of the balloon (like rays coming off the sun) and write on these lines my associations with the word in the circle. For example, I might write "coffee table."inside the circle and then draw lines extending out from the balloon with associations I have with a coffee table.

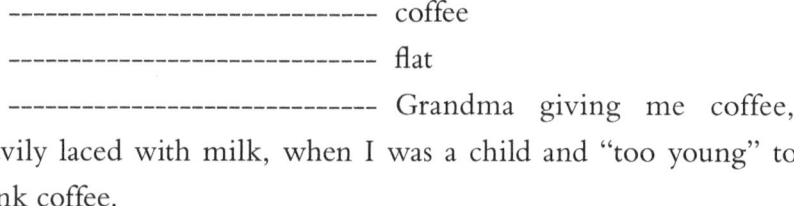

-------------------------------- coffee
-------------------------------- flat
-------------------------------- Grandma giving me coffee, heavily laced with milk, when I was a child and "too young" to drink coffee.

If something doesn't make sense after the first batch of word associations, you can branch off from those words until something strikes you as meaningful.

You might associate coffee, for example, with coughing. A play on words. (Do you need to quit smoking?)

Grandma diluting the coffee may be pointing out that you aren't ready for some "strong" information.

"Flat" (as in table top) may relate to your emotions.

Don't worry about it "making sense." Your subconscious will recognize when you've hit on something.

Is your life feeling flat? Is there something in the "coffee table book" you need to know about? Is there an issue in your living room (life) that you need to pay attention to? Where did the coffee table come from? Did you choose it yourself or was it given to you and you'd rather toss it in the trash but feel obligated to keep it? And is there something else in your life you feel that way about?

The following example comes from a dream in which a woman was transplanting flowers and discovered there were worms in the flowers and they were crawling under her skin. She tried to pull them out but they kept breaking.

Using the balloon method, she began listing things she associated with worms. They were dirty, scary, represented death, were good for fertilizer and were disgusting. "Disgusting" was the key word and she indicated so with an exclamation point. How did she know "disgusting" was what her dream was trying to convey to her? Gut feeling. It felt right. (Dream analysis is more about intuition than science.)

Another symbol involved was the worms getting "under her skin." Using the balloon method, once again, she began writing down a list of things she associated with being "under her skin." Itching, penetrating, and feeling dirty all came up, but what "hit home," for her, was the word "irritating." Thinking about "disgusting" and "irritating," she realized she was letting her husband's criticism "get under her skin" and she was "disgusted" with herself for allowing this to happen.

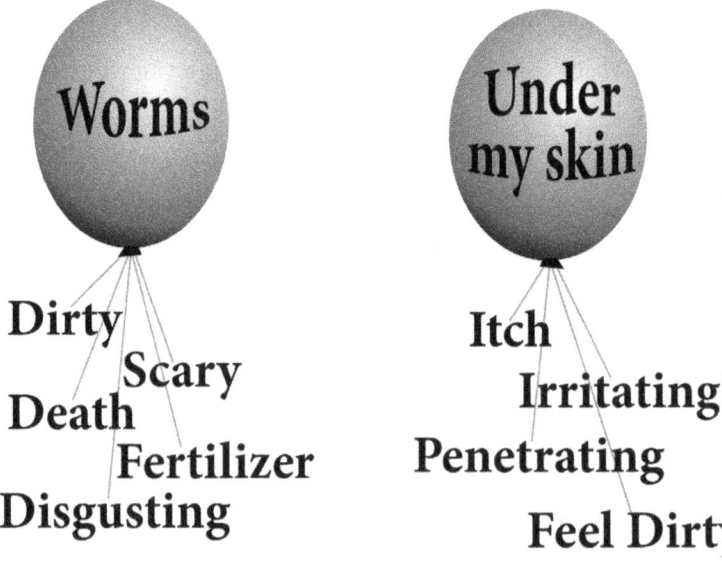

Illustration by Curtis Killorn

Dream analysis is a very individual thing. For a man operating a bait shop, the same symbols would have a totally different meaning. Worms might represent profit and having the worms "under his skin" might indicate his concern about having purchased too many worms that aren't selling and that is getting "under his skin" (irritating him) because he may lose money.

Remember, with dreams, it's all about you! And in this case, that's a good thing...

CHAPTER THREE

Dreams offer colorful solutions

It was once believed people only dreamed in black and white. I don't know where anyone came up with that, because I can't ever remember dreaming in black and white, but it's one of those long-held beliefs that have since been disproved. Indeed, people may have some dreams in black and white but they also dream in color and sometimes in some pretty weird colors so knowing a little about color in dreams will help you decipher the messages that come to you in the dream state.

Colors aren't always "natural" in dreams. Yellow, for example, can be an indication of a liver or gall bladder problem. One dreamer was in a kitchen where everything was yellow; the floor, the walls, the food and even his grandmother who was serving the food. A visit to a doctor a few days later determined he had a gall bladder problem. (Bile is a thick fluid that passes from the bile duct of the liver into the common bile duct and then into the gall bladder. The color can range from yellow to green.)

Sometimes the sky may be green and the grass blue, indicating something "not natural" for you is going on. Generally, anything happening within a structure (usually a house or vehicle) is happening within your body. Things happening outdoors indicate something that is affecting you from an outside influence. For example, a situation not of your doing, may be affecting you physically or emotionally. Someone or something outside yourself may be inducing your stress. So pay attention to where you are in a dream. Are you indoors or out? In a zoo? Things may be "like a zoo" at the office.

Unfortunately, in dealing with stress induced by someone else, the only thing you can really do is change the way you react to the stress because you can't change the other person. But at least realizing the source of the stress will get you on the path to releasing and healing.

A good way to associate color in dreams is to think about what a color commonly means to you. Red may be blood, anger or passion. If red is a favorite color it will have a different meaning for you than if you don't like red. Seeing a lot of red in a kitchen in a dream might indicate a bleeding problem in the digestive area. Seeing a lot of red in the bathroom (the area for elimination) might indicate something like hemorrhoids or blood in the urine that you haven't detected yet on a physical level.

If you are outside and the trees and grass are red it may be an indication of "seeing red" (angry) about something. Going through common associations and expressions can provide a clue to the dream content.

Yellow, in an emotional sense, might indicate a lack of courage about something.

Blue could indicate poor circulation or it could represent feeling "blue." White may indicate infection (as in a friend's dream of someone having "too many white cells" and learning two days later she had an abscessed tooth.)

If everything in a dream is green you might be "green with envy" about something or you may be about to become nauseated.

When my mother-in-law wasn't feeling well she always said her coffee tasted "green."

Green could also indicate being new to something as in "green" on the job. Turn your imagination loose in looking for meanings because dreams have very creative ways of getting the message across.

As luck would have it, as I was writing this chapter on color in dreams, a friend called me with a very vivid dream about colors, which I initially thought was related to a physical problem. As it turned out it involved making a decision and the colors really had nothing to do with it.

Lynn lives in Maine, a cold climate, and in the dream she is wearing one navy blue knit sock and one black knit sock and she is trying to decide which color to wear or if one of each will be okay.

Immediately I thought of poor circulation – the dark color in the extremities – or possibly the temperature in her bedroom being too cold. Neither fit. In fact she had gone to bed with socks on because it was cold and when she woke up after the dream, she took them off because they were too warm. So her dream about socks, at least in part, actually did have a physical connection.

I suggested she might be having a problem making a decision about something, which was actually pretty inconsequential (as indicated in the dream) because one could actually wear one navy blue sock and one black one and chances are no one would ever know the difference. It just wasn't that important.

"That's it," Lynn said. "I've been trying to make up my mind about something and haven't been able to decide and I felt concerned that someone was waiting for me to make up my mind, just like in the dream. The dream was so vivid I can still see those knit socks."

She made her decision, notified the person who was waiting, and hasn't had the dream again.

Colors in dreams may also be related to the chakra colors – the energy centers of the body. There are seven generally recognized chakras. The seventh or crown chakra on the top of the head is purple, the third eye in the center of the forehead is indigo (a kind of blue violet), the throat chakra is blue, the heart chakra is green, the solar plexus is yellow, the abdomen and sexual organs are orange and the base chakra, at the bottom of the spine is red.

Dreaming about one of these colors, especially if in excess (the yellow kitchen and grandmother) may be alerting you to an imbalance in that area of the body.

I have heard reference from time to time of another chakra point, which extends above the head, beyond the body. This chakra is more of a spiritual rather than a physical energy point. I don't recall hearing a name for it, but the colors associated with it are white and gold.

I mention this because sometimes dreams of a spiritual nature may come to you and you can identify them by their colors – white and gold. My most recent experience with this was about two years ago when an elderly family member passed away. I was not particularly close to him because I live in Colorado and he lived in Michigan and he was relatively new to the family, through marriage. However, one early morning George came to me in a dream and he was looking absolutely glowing, dressed in a white suit and standing in front of a bright light that seemed to cause a golden glow, kind of like a full-body halo, around him.

Now George was not a man to wear a suit, much less a white one, but in spite of that I still didn't realize this was a dream.

Surprised to see him, I asked, "George, what are you doing here?

He said, "I came to say goodbye."

About 9:30 the next morning I got a phone call from my mother telling me George had passed away, which, of course, I already knew.

I assured her he was happy and healthy, if you can say healthy applies to a spirit, and I knew this was true because he was very happy and absolutely glowing in the dream. And the colors – white and gold – told me it was a spiritual message.

The mother of a teenage girl revealed another fascinating dream related to chakra color. Denise was concerned about her 17-year-old daughter's behavior and her withdrawn, secretive attitude. She suspected something was wrong, but wasn't sure if it was just "normal" teenage moodiness or something more serious.

The answer came in just a little snippet of a dream in which Denise found herself looking out a big window, which she described as royal blue. (Indigo blue, very similar to royal blue, is the color of the third eye chakra which provides insight and a window indicates an eye or insight.)

She remembered very clearly walking to the window and knowing she was supposed to open it but she couldn't see anything outside. Just the blue window.

The next evening after dinner she happened to be walking by the bathroom when she heard her daughter throwing up. She opened the door and found her daughter sticking her finger down her throat, trying to vomit her dinner.

"As it turned out, she had an eating disorder," Denise said. "That prompted me to bring her to a therapist and the problem is getting resolved."

The blue window represented Denise's third eye chakra, which is related to seeing, both physically and intuitively. The dream was telling this mother to open her eyes and see the problem, which she did, and fortunately she was able to help her daughter before the problem got any worse.

Although Denise wasn't "into" studying and analyzing dreams, this was not the first time a dream had provided her with an answer to a serious question. The other situation was an emotional dilemma that went back to her high school years when she had been dating a young man for about a year. She cared for him deeply.

"I suspected he was cheating on me, but he had everyone lying for him," Denise said. "Even my friends assured me I was imagining things, until one night I dreamed the girl he was dating came to me and told me he was lying."

Denise confronted her boyfriend with the fact that his girlfriend had told her the truth – not revealing it came in a dream. The boyfriend confessed and she ended the relationship.

"From now on I'll pay attention to all my dreams," she said. "Sometimes dreams are like a best friend. They tell you things you don't really want to know but it's for your own good, and when that happens you can do something about the problem."

Another "color" dream of my own assured me my father was still with me, even though he had been dead 12 years at the time. The color didn't relate to any particular chakra but to the fact that my dad loved yellow roses.

On the night of February 28, 2009, I went to bed thinking about my dad because he has passed away on Feb. 29, 1996 – Leap Year Day.

In life he had been positively rigid about doing things the right way and at the right time. For example, if a birthday fell on a Wednesday he insisted it be celebrated on a Wednesday – not on the weekend when it would be more convenient. So when he died it was no surprise to anyone in our family that he chose Leap Year Day to make his exit. My father was the epitome of a family man and he did not want his family to suffer, so even though he'd been in a coma, following a stroke, for a couple of weeks, we had no doubt he chose Feb. 29 to make his exit to make it easier on the family. That way we would only have a "real" anniversary of his death every four years.

So on Feb. 28, 2009 when I saw my dad in a dream, I asked him if he would show me a yellow rose within the next couple of days, if he were still around. He said he would and I remembered that and wrote it in my dream journal, knowing full well there wasn't much of a chance of finding a yellow rose in Colorado in February.

About two days later I attended the funeral of a friend. The picture on the front of the program was a yellow rose. There was a spray of yellow roses on her casket and I learned yellow roses had been her favorite flower. Then the minister picked up one of the yellow roses and began walking around the church handing out approximately 10 petals from the yellow rose as she eulogized about my friend. In a church of about 150 people I received one of the petals. Next we go to the graveside service at the cemetery where the minister invited everyone to take a flower from the arrangement on the casket and handed me a single yellow rose to get the ball rolling.

My dad kept his word – even in a dream.

Black and white dreams, however, are not without merit. If a repetitive dream has been in color and then becomes black and white it is an indication that the issue that is prompting the dream has become less significant. Since dreams are the body/mind/spirit's way of working out problems and stresses during our sleeping hours, whenever one is plagued by vivid nightmares and dreams, it may be helpful to ask, before retiring, for the dream or nightmare to come in black and white and thus tone down the emotions a bit.

CHAPTER FOUR

Setting the Scene for our Dreaming

To dream, one must first get to sleep, so the person seriously interested in dream studies needs first to make sure his/her place of sleep is conducive to getting a good night's rest.

Having a good, comfortable mattress is important. Buy the best you can afford, in whatever firmness feels good to you. One of my daughters is most comfortable sleeping on the floor with just a blanket and pillow. The hard surface actually supports her "bad back" and allows her to rest more comfortably. Others are in their comfort zone in a beanbag chair or a soft feather bed.

If your bedroom is also your living space you might find it difficult to switch your mind-set to thoughts of sleep if your bed is the living room couch or if you've been using your bed as a table, to cut patterns on or as a place to study.

Ideally there should not be a TV in the bedroom. If there is, watch it from a chair or the floor. Program your mind to think of bed, sleep and dreams as synonymous.

Your bed should be your own personal space, not to be invaded by anyone other than the partner you may be sharing it with, and your dreams.

If possible, don't even read in bed. Sit in a chair in your bedroom or at a desk. Reading my lull you to sleep and again, the content of your dreams may reflect what you were reading. There are times when that may be desirable, like when you are studying or reading a self-help book, but in general, keep all activities other than sleep and sex, off the bed.

Keep noise to a minimum. I know many people who feel they have to have a TV or a radio on all night to sleep, but doing this defeats the purpose if you want to have those marvelous dream adventures. As with reading and then falling asleep, sometimes the content of the TV or radio can infiltrate your dreams, creating more of a challenge for you when you try to figure them out.

Of course there are exceptions to everything. The early sleep state when the brain is in the alpha state is when the subconscious is most susceptible to learning. It's the same state a person is in when they are in hypnotic trance. It's not "sleep" but rather a totally relaxed state of mind where the subconscious is open to accepting suggestion. Your subconscious is like a sponge in this state, ready to absorb information. So during that span of time, just before you fall asleep is the perfect time to play learning tapes if you are trying to learn another language, listening to a book on tape, etc. This is also the time to play self-hypnosis tapes if you are trying to accomplish something like smoking cessation or weight loss.

This alpha stage-one sleep is also the stage where we drift off into dreams. The difference in the "drifting off" sleep and actual dream sleep is called REM or Rapid Eye Movement sleep. When we are in the dream state, our eyes move rapidly, as though we are watching a movie on the back of our eyelids. You may have observed this, especially if you have children or pets. The amount of REM sleep we experience decreases with age.

It has been proposed that the high percentage of REM sleep is necessary for appropriate maturation and activation of the young child's brain: the REM percentage for children decreases by about the fourth year to the level found in adults. (Our Dreaming Mind, Robert L. Van De Castle, Ph.D., Ballantine Books, NY, 1994).

We have all heard the expression to "sleep on it" when contemplating a solution to a problem. I was surprised to find there was actually some validity to that. A friend, an attorney, tells me he sleeps on his briefs prior to going to court and somehow he absorbs the information and is better prepared for his day in court. It's certainly not scientifically provable but I have no reason to doubt him. In fact I was a bit surprised to hear him admit to it, but it makes perfect sense to me. There are so many things in life we don't understand but that doesn't mean they aren't real. Do you understand how a light bulb works? Or how an aspirin knows how to find it's way to a headache? Me neither, but it works.

When fully alert, the brain waves are cycling at 14 to 30 per second. In the alpha state they are cycling at 8 to 13 per second. The other levels of sleep are theta (4 to 7 cycles per second) which ranges from drowsiness to unconscious, and delta (.05 to 3.5 cycles per second) which is a very deep sleep state. (New Age Hypnosis, Dr. Bruce Goldberg, Llewellyn Publications, 1999).

Delta level sleep, while it is a non – REM sleep, continues to provide learning experiences at deeper levels. These include lessons for overall spiritual growth and development. At times you may even recall a glimpse of being in a school, college or some other learning place from the delta state. (The Mystical, Magical, Marvelous World of Dreams, Wilda B. Tanner, Sparrow Hawk Press, 2001.) In general, dreamers don't recall dreams from the delta state but these are the deep level dreams that result in a person suddenly realizing they have discovered a solution to a problem they have been concerned about for some time - that "why didn't I think of that before?" feeling.

The reason you didn't think of it before is because you hadn't processed the situation in your dream world. Once that is done, "Dr. Dream" provides us with solutions that pleasantly surprise us with answers to seemingly impossible problems.

If you are serious about working with your dreams, make your bedroom as comfortable as possible. Something you might want to adopt from a Native American tradition is to hang a dream catcher above your bed. A dream catcher isn't just a pretty wall ornament. In case you're not familiar with them, they are usually in the form of a circle with a web of string inside the frame that looks like a spider web with a hole in the center.

The idea behind the dream catcher is that it catches the important messages from your dreams so they won't be lost. The bad dreams are supposed to drop through the hole in the center.

It's important that the dream catcher be yours and yours alone. Never bring home a dream catcher unless it's from someone you know and trust and even then, cleanse it by leaving it out in the sun or under the full moon for three days or nights.

I once was asked to investigate a house that was supposedly haunted. This can happen at times, when the energy of a person who died suddenly continues to linger in a dwelling, not realizing he/she is dead and therefore, not wanting to or being afraid to move into the light. Probably the most frequent example of this is a suicide or a sudden accident. At any rate, once the lingering spirit can be convinced to move on, things improve for the current resident. (For more information on this read The Unquiet Dead by Dr. Edith Fiore, Ballantine Books, 1987.) There are also many other books on the market about spirit possession that may be helpful.

Anyway, the woman who was renting this particular house had a long list of bad things that had happened to herself and her family, plus there was a general negative feeling about the house and she wanted it gone.

After spending about a half-hour in the house, I could find nothing to indicate a problem, I apologized for not being able to help and was headed out the door when a large gray and tan dream catcher, hanging on the wall behind a chair, caught my eye. The feeling that hit me was so strong it was like someone threw a pail of cold water on me.

"Where did you get that?" I asked. The dream catcher was mostly gray feathers and beige colored woven straw with some beads and crystals woven into it and a couple of feathers hanging off the bottom, but for some reason it felt positively formidable.

The woman smiled. "I got it at a yard sale," she said. "Isn't it pretty? I was just drawn to it…."

"Get rid of it," I said. "That's where your problem is coming from." It was one of those gut-feeling situations. I just knew I was right.

She insisted she couldn't do that. She loved the dream catcher. I, on the other hand, couldn't get out of the house fast enough.

I never saw her again, so I don't know if the situation in her house changed or not but I truly hope she got rid of the dream catcher because it was definitely carrying a negative energy.

If you want to catch dreams, make sure they are your own.

CHAPTER FIVE

Dream Enhancers

Sitting alone at a psychic fair in Crestone, Colorado, I watched the visitors pass my booth and go on to the Tarot card readers, the candle booths, the massage therapists and the other practitioners who had "something to offer."

The few people who did stop to chat, probably because they felt sorry for the poor dream analyst sitting there all alone, all said the same thing; I don't remember my dreams or I don't dream. Therefore, I had nothing to offer them. We'd chat for a while and I'd assure them that yes, everybody does dream, but everybody doesn't remember their dreams. Then I'd offer a few hints about enhancing sleep to help to induce dreams, and a little information to help them remember their dreams and they would thank me and go on to the next booth.

It was at that point I decided I was no longer going to set up a booth for dream analysis at psychic fairs. Instead, I would devote my time to classes teaching people how to induce, enhance, program, and ultimately remember their dreams so they could take advantage of this marvelous subconscious teacher that is within us all.

Many native cultures, Native Americans among them, advocate fasting before attempting to induce a dream. In ancient Greece, when people visited temples honoring the Greek god of medicine, Aesculapius, in the hope of inducing dreams to answer their problems; they fasted before preparing to receive an answer in their dreams. They also prayed and offered sacrifices to Aesculapius in the hope that he would come to them in dreams and prescribe cures for their illness.

I haven't delved into the benefits of fasting vs. not fasting when trying to induce a dream, but as just about everyone already knows (and many have experienced), if you eat a heavy meal that taxes your digestive system before going to bed, chances are you're going to have some pretty strange dreams and they may not be of the sort that solves problems for you. On the other hand, going to bed overly hungry may not induce the type of dream that will answer questions either. You will probably end up dreaming of roast turkey, pizza and cheesecake.

When I was very ill for two years from the side effects of the antibiotic I mentioned earlier, I was too sick to hold down much food. During that time, one of my most vivid dreams, in this hungry state, was of sitting at a table and seeing a plate of fluffy mashed potatoes with rich brown gravy, just out of my reach. Placed in front of me was my "dinner" – a big plate of purple pills. Now there's a dream that doesn't take any work to analyze. I was craving comfort food but the only "nurturing" I was getting was in the form of medications, one of which actually was a purple pill.

A psychic I met several years ago, whose name I no longer recall, once mentioned something about food that has stayed with me over the years. She said the white powders of sugar, salt and bleached white flour are just as bad as the white powder of cocaine for a person who wants to be clear and receptive to psychic work. I would think that would also apply to dream work since we are working with the subconscious. So avoid these "white powders" as much as possible if you are serious about seeking answers in your dreams. Besides, they aren't really healthy anyway.

Having your bedroom at a comfortable temperature is important. Too hot and you may dream of slashing your way through a jungle or being in a hot tub. Too cold and you may dream of being in Antarctica or some cold place where you actually have been. Our surroundings definitely affect our dreams.

Don't drink alcohol before going to bed. Alcohol is a depressant and may adversely affect your dreams. I know some people claim a small glass of wine before bedtime helps them to sleep and since I haven't tried that, I can't say it isn't true, but too much is definitely not a good thing and it will affect your dreams, just like some medications will affect dreams.

About the best sleep aid I've tried is taking one 5HTP capsule (a type of tryptophan) and one melatonin capsule at bedtime. (Tryptophan is the stuff that's in turkey that makes you want to sack out on the couch after Thanksgiving dinner.) It's worked for me and others I know and it's not affected our dreams when taken occasionally. They should not be taken long-term (more than a couple of months) without taking some time off. And of course, always consult a health care practitioner before doing this, especially if taking a prescription drug or if pregnant or nursing. Taking the two together, melatonin and 5HTP together seems to be the secret. I have heard adverse reports of "weird dreams" from people taking just the melatonin.

Physical problems that are coming on or already with us are also manifested in dreams in ways that are related to the problem we are experiencing. Months before I was diagnosed with asthma back in 1978 I would awaken in the early morning from various types of "suffocation dreams." Sometimes I'd be drowning. Sometimes I'd be dreaming the pillow was in my face. Once I was in an avalanche and covered with snow. (The heat had gone out.) Then I'd wake up and find I was having moderate difficulty breathing. That moderate difficulty escalated over the next few months until on March 15, 1978 I had a near death experience from an asthma attack. Looking back on that experience, that was the turning point when I decided to make major changes in my life. We moved from Michigan to Colorado when I was told I had six months to live if I didn't get to a warmer, dryer climate. What that warmer, dryer climate also provided, aside from escaping from the cold and humid weather, was an awakening to alternative healing, dream study, and further pursuit of studies in hypnotherapy that would never had happened had I remained "at home" in Michigan where I had lived for 38 years. Those "suffocation" dreams were the first step to a new life for me.

Smells can also affect our dreams, so if possible, allow some fresh air to enter your sleeping space before bedtime, ridding it of cooking odors, cleaning smells or any strong smells that might influence your dreams.

Pleasant smells, on the other hand, may help induce restful sleep. Bed and bath shops often have aromatic sleep pillows filled with herbs such as lavender and chamomile that will help induce sleep. A dab of lavender or chamomile essential oil on the pillowcase or in the bath water may help induce sleep.

If you live in an area where you may be bothered by traffic or other noise, block out distracting noises by wearing earplugs, putting cotton in your ears or by playing New Age music or something like Mozart. Author Don Campbell, in his book, "The Mozart Effect," (Avon Books, 1997) extols the benefits of listening to classical music when doing healing work. "White noise," like a humidifier or fan may also help if you need to cover up traffic sounds or noise from an adjacent apartment.

Keeping the room dark aids sleep. Eliminate nightlights, if possible, unless there is danger of you or someone else falling during the night. And if you go to bed early or know the early morning sun will be shining in your window when you still want to sleep, get some dark, heavy curtains or try one of those sleep masks like they sometimes provide on airplanes. Early morning dreams are often the most fruitful in terms of providing you with information, so you especially don't want that dreamtime interrupted.

To enhance sleep and dreams, it's important to get some exercise during the day, especially in the fresh air. Something as simple as a walk around the block, a bike ride or a short swim early in the evening is always helpful. On the other hand, too much exercise late in the evening, like weight lifting and aerobics, can be detrimental to sleep. This will rev up your metabolism and keep you "wired" and you'll have difficulty mellowing out and going to sleep.

Many people who work with dreams cite the benefits of crystals to enhance the dream state. Here again, it's a case of "different strokes for different folks." Some swear by the benefit of crystals. Others see them only as pretty rocks. I personally haven't used crystals in working with my dreams but I know many people, whose opinions I value, who would not be without them. Do they "work"? I don't know. But I also don't know how an electric light bulb works, or how an aspirin know how to go to the right place to cure a headache.

Quartz crystals come in many different colors and target all the chakras, which are the energy centers of the body. Rose quartz opens the heart area and allows loving energies to manifest. It heals wounds of the emotions. Smoky quartz is for grounding and channels energies to help one become balanced and grounded and may help to alleviate anxiety or panic attacks, which can be detrimental to sleep. Clear quartz crystals are probably the best "all purpose" crystal to use for attracting and enhancing dreams because they work with the full spectrum of energy and can be programmed for pretty much any purpose. Just do a little research, pick a small crystal you determine the best for the problem at hand, and hold it in your hand or put it in your pillowcase when you retire for the night.

Jessica Saunders, a master crystal healer with The Gathering Place…a Center for Wellness in Salida, Colorado, studied under Katrina Raphaell, author of "Crystal Enlightenment – The Transforming Properties of Crystals and Healing Stones" (Aurora Press, NY, 1985) and "Crystal Healing – The Therapeutic Application of Crystals and Stones" (Aurora Press, 1987) and finds fluorite to be helpful with dream work. Fluorite is believed to help concentration, and meditation and to help the holder grasp abstract concepts. It also facilitates communications between dimensions.

Fluorite can be used to help resolve both physical and emotional problems but it is especially good for physical ailments. And you don't need a large, expensive crystal.

"Anything from a little octahedron to a big chunk will work, " Jessica says. Crystals work in conjunction with the different chakras, which are the energy centers of the body, and fluorite is associated with the "third eye" chakra, which is located in the center of the forehead. The third eye is associated with spiritual insight. Fluorite comes in a variety of colors, blue, purple, gold and white as well as multicolor, which is Jessica's preference when working with dreams.

Moonstone is another favorite of Jessica's, particularly blue moonstone, although it also comes in gray and yellow. Moonstone helps the holder eliminate old emotional patterns and often this can be done through the dream state.

"For the beginner just starting to work with crystals to induce dreams, I would recommend the blue moonstone," Jessica says. "I put it in my pillowcase or hold it in my hand and as soon as I wake up I record the dream and as soon as possible, interpret it so I don't lose the information and the feeling of the dream."

Emerald is another stone known for healing qualities but the price of an emerald scares people off.

"Not to worry," Jessica says. "You can often find what I call "crumbs" of precious stones like emeralds, diamonds and rubies, especially if you know someone who cuts stones. You don't need a cut and polished stone. Those crumbs will work. I just put them in a small plastic baggie to keep them together and sometimes I put them in an additional cloth bag the color of the stone."

Rev. Joseph Richards, who does spirit guided readings in Salida, Colorado recommends obsidian for dream work but adds, it should be used with caution.

"Obsidian goes into the subconscious," he said. "I recommend not starting with obsidian but progressing up to it, starting with a small piece, about the size of a penny. Snowflake obsidian (black and white) is good to start with and one with other colors is preferable to all black."

Obsidian is generally associated with black but there are many other colors including those with blue, silver and gold sheens as well as some with mahogany streaks.

"For serious physical and emotional problems I would use obsidian, but with caution," Jessica said. "Obsidian tends to drop you back into the physical state quickly. It doesn't ease you back in."

She recommends blue as the most calming, to be used with milder problems and particularly for emotional problems.

For physical problems, start with mahogany which is oxidized magnetite and/or hematite, often contained in black obsidian.

"I've been playing with stones for 50 years," Jessica said, "and one thing I've found is that crystals are called different names in different areas. So if you are using stones for healing and dream work, make sure you have the right stones."

She recommends the books by Katrina Raphaell and Melodie as excellent resources. Melodie's most recent book in her "Love Is In the Earth" series, (Earth – Love Publishing House, Wheatridge, CO, 2008) is a comprehensive volume including all crystals as of 2009, their colors and components along with photographs to help the reader determine if he/she has the right stone. New crystals and minerals are being discovered all the time.

"The important thing is to find the right stone in the right color and check out its properties in a crystal guide book," Jessica said. "Sometimes crystal and New Age shop owners are very knowledgeable, but other times not and when they are not, you need a good book to guide you."

Other good and much less expensive books Jessica recommends are Crystal & Gemstone Divination by Gail Butler, The Illustrated Directory of Healing Stones by Cassandra Eason and Minerals of the World by Walter Schumann.

CHAPTER SIX

Deciphering

While things like crystals and essential oils may enhance dream work, minimal equipment is actually needed in working with dreams to help diagnose and treat physical and emotional problems. As mentioned previously, a good dream dictionary is certainly helpful and I would even say, necessary, especially in the beginning. Along with that you'll need a pen and paper or a small tape or digital recorder, preferably a hand-held one, to write or record your dreams. Keep your notebook or recorder on a bedside table, or, if this isn't practical because you'll disturb your mate, keep the equipment in the bathroom.

Start with a specific goal or problem you want to work on so you can program your dreams before you go to bed. To do this, come up with a seven-syllable suggestion or question and repeat that command at least three times before letting yourself drift off to sleep.

A good general idea is to focus on the problem before going to sleep and then tell yourself three times – a dream will bring the answer. (Count 'em. Seven syllables.) More specific might be "Shall I ac-cept this new job?" Or "How do I heal my asth-ma?"

Sometimes it takes a little work condensing your goal into seven syllables, but in working with the statement, you also serve a purpose. As you focus on the wording, the suggestion is working into your subconscious even as you strive to phrase it properly.

You may not remember your dreams the first night or even the first few nights. Or if you do, they may seem to have nothing to do with what you are trying to find out. But trust me. It will happen.

Keep that dream dictionary close at hand, but before we get started, here are a few very basic symbols to keep in mind.

Buildings represent your body or your state of consciousness. If you are inside the building the "problem" is within yourself, like a problem with self-esteem. If you are outside the building, it indicates something outside yourself, like someone else giving you grief! And be aware of the type of building, the condition it's in and where it's located. All of these provide you with clues you can use in deciphering your dream.

A school, for example, would indicate a learning experience; a church, something spiritual; the home where you grew up, something from the past.

The rooms in a house symbolize different parts of your body or different aspects of yourself. Are you in the bathroom, on the toilet? You may need to eliminate something in your life. In the kitchen? Perhaps you need to nurture yourself. In the basement? You may be dealing with a subconscious element you aren't aware of yet. Or you may be having a problem with something in the "bottom" of your body, usually the feet and legs, since the organs of elimination are usually represented by the bathroom and a need to eliminate.

A very common dream is finding rooms in a house that you didn't know were there. This indicates hidden talents or abilities you are either not yet aware of or haven't explored for one reason or another.

In the early years of my marriage we lived in a tiny one-bedroom house with two children. During those years I had a repetitive dream of going into the closet and finding a small secret door through which I miraculously entered a whole other spacious house, right down to a baby grand piano and library in the living room. When I began to seriously study dreams I remembered that one, which I had originally attributed to a desire to have more much needed space. But at the same time in my life, I was undergoing an emotional struggle, typical of young mothers, where I was unable to utilize the talents I had because my life was so busy. The other rooms, complete with a piano and books, I believe, represented the talents that remained "hidden" because I could not utilize them at that point in my life when I was so busy with my family. And possibly, it may have been a little of both – dreaming of more room and being unable to use my "hidden" talents.

Parts of buildings may also correspond to parts of bodies. Windows may represent eyes. Pulling shades down may indicate not wanting to see something or possibly having a problem with eyesight. Doors may represent body openings. Pregnant women, even before they know they are pregnant, will often dream of adding bay windows or porches onto a house or of putting something "in the oven."

Vehicles represent physical bodies. Note the type of vehicle and how it applies to you. Is it the car your father drove, a dump truck or an airplane? Are you afraid of big, noisy vehicles? (Perhaps big noisy people scare you too! Are there any big, noisy people in your life that you are afraid of?)

Did you hate Sunday afternoon rides as a kid because you got carsick? All of these factor into what the symbol means for you.

Are you "in the driver's seat?" If so, you are in charge of the situation. But if you are the passenger or in the back seat you may be being "taken for a ride." Also be aware of the direction the vehicle is moving. Is it moving forward? Fast or slow? Are there curves in the road or detours? (Curves thrown at you in life or detours you may have been forced, or chose, to take.) Is it going in reverse or stuck?

Airplanes are worth a special mention here because airplanes generally indicate a spiritual "taking off." Going to the airport or being in an airplane may signify a spiritual awakening.

Bicycles symbolize balance. Are you trying to balance too many things? Home, kids, job, etc.? This can contribute to emotional stress and physical illness.

Water represents emotion. Be aware if the water is quiet and peaceful, turbulent, stagnant, etc. Water symbolizes how you are feeling in general or about a specific situation.

Weather may also represent emotions. Watch for stormy, cold, dry and barren landscapes, etc. and ask yourself how they apply to your emotions.

Plants and their condition in a dream may indicate the condition of your body. Patricia Garfield, Ph.D., a gardener and author of books on dreams, knows when her physical health is deteriorating because the plants in her dreams become droopy or infected.

People are almost always aspects of you, the exception being if you are working on a concern about a relationship. In that case the person in your dreams may actually represent that individual.

Males usually represent a conscious aspect of yourself – something you already know but may have not wanted to acknowledge, so if the man in your dreams is your father, be aware of what attributes you associate with your father. Was he honest, reliable, a control freak, etc.? If the male is a famous person, like President Obama, what qualities do you associate with him? Are they qualities you have, wish you had or wish you didn't have? Ask yourself how does this relate to me?

If female, do you have an aggressive side you don't want to acknowledge? Or do you wish you were more aggressive?

Females in a dream represent unconscious aspects of yourself or the more nurturing side of yourself – parts of you that you are not aware of. So if you dream of your cousin, Sue, and you consider her a bitch on wheels, better take a closer look at yourself and see if maybe those qualities apply to you.

Males dreaming of females may be seeing their feminine or nurturing side. I once had a client who was concerned because in a dream he was dressed as a female. Happily married, he wasn't the least bit inclined to be homosexual or even bisexual but the dream really freaked him out until he realized it was his new career as a nurse that was causing him to relate to the feminine/nurturing side of himself.

Just be aware of the attributes of the particular female or male in the dream.

Sex in a dream doesn't mean you are fantasizing about having sex with your favorite teacher, your cousin, or the letter carrier. In general, dreaming of having sex, being "in bed" with someone, getting married or other symbols of union, indicate the uniting of the conscious and the subconscious. What was previously unconscious is emerging into your level of awareness.

Take a dream of having sex with your cousin, for example. Not to worry about incest. Instead, look at the attributes of that person. Is he/she successful in business, an accomplished musician or an outspoken critic? Having sex or marrying that cousin may be pointing out your desire to "unite" with those qualities.

Food indicates a desire or need to nurture oneself.

These are just a few of the really basic symbols you are likely to encounter once you start picking apart the symbols in your dreams.

Once you wake up from a dream, particularly if you were able to induce that dream by suggestion, take a minute or two before you get out of bed to replay it in your mind. Make note of who was in the dream, the colors, numbers, vehicles, whether you were indoors or outdoors, what kind of a building you were in, what type of outdoor area you were in (forest, desert, home where you grew up, etc.), any words or phrases that were spoken and any feelings you experienced. Sometimes the smallest symbol, like a bug (something "bugging you") is the one that will provide the key to the answer you seek. Numbers may be a clue to a month, age, year, etc. so check a dream dictionary for the significance of particular numbers, bearing in mind that large numbers may need to be reduced to a single number to find an answer. Very basically, numerology involves reducing numbers to a single number. For example, the number 251 would be reduced by adding 2 plus 5 plus 1 to make 8. If the total ends in two or three digits, you continue to reduce. For example, the number 82 would be reduced by adding 8 plus 2 equals 10 and then 1 plus 0 equals one.

Now, having replayed the dream in your mind, either sit up in bed or go to a nearby room (I use the bathroom), and record your dream or write it down. If possible, do this in a dim light, such as a night-light. Rather than shedding light on the subject, turning on a bright light sometimes causes details of the dream to disappear.

First, jot down or verbally list the symbols you remember. For example, in the dream that follows, I would list the symbols – Chicago, late, yard sale, muddy road, man, Annette. By jotting down the symbols quickly, you are more likely to remember all or most of the details than if you begin by writing a narrative of the dream.

My dream is this: I am going to Chicago and I'm late for a yard sale. The road is a detour and it is very muddy. A man in green puts his hand on my shoulder and asks if I mind and says it is good that I do this on my own. People are in a line but I don't know why. An older woman I know (Annette) is among them.

Writing the narrative can wait until morning once you have captured the essence in your dream with this list. If the dream was interesting enough and you want it to continue, go back to bed and tell yourself – my dream will con-tin-ue now. (Seven syllables). If not, just go back to bed. You can figure out the dream in the morning.

Often the dream seems to make no sense at all, but trust me – it will. And it gets easier with practice.

Write the narrative as soon as possible after getting up. It's a good idea to make a habit of doing that first thing in the morning, before you do anything else. Always date your dreams and, since you may have several dreams during the night, number them. For example, June 2, 2008, #1. It's also helpful and actually kind of fun to give your dream a title, like a story. My dream, above, might be "A Trip To Chicago" or simply "Chicago."

There is something about giving them a title that also makes them easier to remember if, in the future, you want to look back in your journal for information. You might also want to list the intensity of the feeling of the dream, especially if you woke up feeling really disturbed, sad, happy, etc. A nice way I've seen this done is to draw a little thermometer and indicate the intensity of your feelings as the mercury rising up in the thermometer. If you're really organized, you might even make an index listing the titles of your dreams and the page they are on.

You may want to write the final analysis in a separate notebook from the one in which you make your original notes. Often those middle-of-the-night notes are pretty difficult to read anyway, so it's good to do them over again more legibly for future reference.

Dating your dreams is important because in the future you will want to note the progress you have made in resolving your problem. For example, a person just beginning to journal his/her dreams might have a health problem of some kind. A sinus problem is a good example. Early dreams may have the dreamer in a messy attic in a dilapidated house. (The messy attic would indicate a "mess" or congestion in the head and the dilapidated house indicates not feeling well or being in poor condition.)

Subsequent dreams may place the dreamer in the same attic trying to clean up the mess, but never quite getting it done. Eventually, though, the dreamer will get the mess picked up and things put into boxes or on shelves. Finally, the dreamer may find the attic is cleaned up and perhaps there is a playroom or office or other useable space in its place.

This sequence of dreams indicates progress toward a goal – cleaning up the sinus infection. Working out a problem, symbolically or otherwise, in a dream, actually does spill over into the waking state.

Okay – I know you are wondering about the Chicago dream. Right? So let's get back to the process of picking apart the symbols and them putting them together to find the meaning of this nocturnal message.

Dream dictionaries are helpful, but the bottom line is – what does the symbol mean to you?

I have never been to Chicago, other than passing through the airport, so what "going to Chicago" means to me will be very different than for someone who was born and raised there, misses it a lot, and has lived in New York for several years.

This is how I deciphered my dream symbols:

Going to Chicago – going to an unknown place, a little scary, since I have always lived in small towns.

Late for a yard sale – late for acquiring some old things. (Things I maybe should have done or learned in the past.)

Muddy road – The "path" I'm taking to reach some goal is difficult.

Detour – I have gotten off the main road but I'm still headed toward my goal.

A man – Conscious aspect of myself.

Green – For me this is a favorite color. Also, in dream work it symbolizes healing and growth.

Statement – "It is good I am doing this on my own." (Self-explanatory)

People in line – Aspects of myself waiting for something. (Since I associate being "in line" with waiting.)

Annette (female) – A female usually represents subconscious aspects of the self, whether you are male or female. Since Annette is an older woman I respect and admire but don't really know very well, she probably represents the older, wiser aspect of myself. (I may be ready to acknowledge the "wiser" part but I'm not so sure I want to acknowledge that "older" part yet!)

Now, looking back over the notes, do you see a story emerging? I am headed in an unfamiliar direction, realizing there are things I should have done in the past that I did not do and it is perhaps too late to do them now. The road I'm traveling is difficult and I've gotten off the beaten path, but I am still headed in the right direction – to Chicago (that unfamiliar place).

A male, in a dream, is usually a conscious aspect of one's self, showing you something you are already aware of. This man, in green, indicates I am healing and growing and he is telling me something I am already consciously aware of – "it is good that you do this on your own."

I picked this dream at random from several dream journals. This one was dated June 1, 2007. At that time, I had just had surgery for nasal polyps (healing). I was still not feeling well and was exploring other ways of healing my chronic allergies (things from the past, since I've had allergies all my life). The dream indicated I was headed in the right direction, even though the going was rough. I was waiting (in line) for something to happen (a cure) and my older, wiser self was with me, perhaps as a guide.

How do I know this is right? Gut feeling. And for the most part, that is how you will know you have analyzed your dream correctly. You just feel it!

You work with the symbols, write down what feels "right" for you and you will know when you get that "aha!" feeling.

I know. It's not very scientific, but that's the way it works. There have been a lot of scientific studies on dreams and if you are so inclined, you can delve into them, as I have done. But the bottom line is, if the meaning you attach to a symbol feels right for you, then it's probably accurate. So trust your judgment and go with it.

CHAPTER SEVEN

Pay Attention to the Signs

Using dreams to diagnose and treat physical and emotional problems can be a very valuable health care tool, but unfortunately, not many physicians are willing to recognize it. However, being unwilling to acknowledge it doesn't mean at least some of them don't pay attention to dreams.

While writing my doctoral dissertation on "Using Dreams to Diagnose and Treat Physical and Emotional Problems," one of the physicians I interviewed, a surgeon, said he definitely did pay attention when a patient mentioned having a dream about his/her health problem or surgery, "But," he added, with a smile, "don't you dare quote me on that."

So I didn't. But I share this just to make the reader aware that there are physicians who do pay attention to this stuff and if you've had a disturbing dream you feel is related to your health or an upcoming medical procedure, it would be worth at least mentioning it to your doctor. The worst he/she can do is ignore it, but maybe – just maybe – it might be helpful.

Dr. Bernie Siegel, retired clinical professor of surgery at Yale New Haven Hospital, has been studying the effects of the mind on the body and vice versa for many years and has written several books on self-healing. Probably the best known is his first book, written in 1986, "Love, Medicine & Miracles." That event redirected his life and he went on to write other books, with the goal of humanizing medical education and medical care as well as empowering patients and teaching survival behavior to enhance immune system competency.

In his work, he has witnessed patients whose dreams forecast physical illness. For example, a patient with breast cancer dreamed her head was shaved and the word cancer written on it. She awoke with the knowledge her cancer had spread to her brain, even though no physical signs or symptoms were present. Three weeks later, the diagnosis was confirmed.

However, a word of caution here – dreaming about cancer does not necessarily mean the dreamer or someone close to him/her has cancer. Think about it. What is cancer? It's a growth! So at times, a dream of cancer could have the positive meaning of growth. It's back to that "gut feeling" again. What do YOU think the dream meant? However, having a dream like the one mentioned above would certainly warrant a visit to your doctor because, as we all know, the earlier we act on a warning the more likely we are to correct it. Early warning signals are best heeded.

When I was working on my dream studies, my friend, Charlene, volunteered to keep a journal of her dreams and share them with me. One of those dreams was particularly interesting. Charlene and I had actually worked together at the local hospital and in this dream she and I and one of the doctors were discussing a patient. The doctor told Charlene the patient had too many white cells.

Usually everyone in a dream represents some aspect of the self, so my interpretation of the dream was that Charlene had an infection somewhere in her body.

"You're pretty good at this," she laughed, "but I'm afraid you're wrong on this one. I'm feeling fine."

Three days later Charlene called to let me know she had an abscessed tooth!

Often, even before women know they are pregnant, they will become aware of that fact in their dreams. One common dream symbol indicating pregnancy is having something "in the oven." A woman might dream of baking and waiting for the item to emerge from the oven. Another pregnancy symbol is an alteration to a house in a dream. The dreamer may find herself adding on a porch or a bay window.

Calvin S. Hall and Robert L. Van de Castle researched dream content analysis from roughly 1947 until 1994. In their book, "Our Dreaming Mind," with some emphasis on pregnant women, the authors mention one young woman hoping to become pregnant, who dreamed of an open shoebox. Suddenly a kitten jumped into the box and the sides folded over by themselves, forming a zipper that held the kitten inside. She could feel the frightened kitten beating against the side of the box. Later, she learned she had become pregnant just about the time she experienced that dream.

Dreams are our body's way of telling us what's going on within. You've probably experienced this yourself, or know someone who has. You have a "feeling" something is wrong and you go to a doctor and he/she asks what makes you think that you have a certain problem or that something is wrong. You say you have a "feeling" and he/she laughs it off and says you read too many magazines, spend too much time on the Internet, or watch too many health shows on TV. But ultimately what you suspected turns out to be true.

If you have a doctor like that, find a new doctor. Your body is just that. YOUR body. No one is more familiar with it than you are. When you experience a physical pain, it gets the attention of your doctor. But when you experience a "feeling" that something is wrong, often such is not the case. You may be sent home with a prescription for an anti-anxiety medication.

I refer again here to my experience with the antibiotic that left me practically unable to function for two years. The first night after taking it I passed out and was taken to the Emergency Room and hospitalized overnight. I was dismissed the next morning and told there was "nothing wrong" but I knew it wasn't over. The next two years of nausea, pain, brain fog, insomnia and other ailments proved me right. Even though medical tests showed "nothing wrong" something was definitely wrong within and it took two years of working at it, mostly with alternative healing methods, to recover. Were it not for the dream I mentioned earlier, about clawing my way to the top of the hill with the dead and dying pumpkins, and then reaching the top and seeing the other side where there were big, beautiful pumpkins as far as the eye could see, I may have given up. But that dream told me there was hope of healing.

While working on my dissertation, I asked several people to share their dreams with me. That group included 11 women, ages 8 to 81, and three men, ages 30 to 79. All had kept records of their dreams over periods of time ranging from one to seven years.

A few of these folks recalled having had dreams about going to the hospital before they actually developed a health problem. Of course, dreaming of going to a hospital doesn't always mean you will go to the hospital. It could simply indicate a desire and a willingness to accept healing, and of course, if you work in a hospital, it could be a direct message about something involving your job during the day, which is processing itself in your dreams at night.

Dreams are a stress reliever. Their purpose is to help people release their stress in their sleep. In fact, dreams are critical to mental and emotional health and even those who claim not to dream are actually working through their feelings in their sleep, even if they don't remember it. But just think how much more valuable that information could be if brought to a conscious level so you can utilize it. Therein lies the purpose of dream analysis. Don't let this valuable form of counseling go to waste. Promise yourself when you go to bed each night that you will remember your dreams and immediately upon awakening, write them down, as mentioned earlier. It takes some time, but eventually you'll find your dreams advising you like a good friend. The only difference is, it might be like having a friend who speaks Russian and you speak English! So for a while, you'll need an interpreter. That would be your dream dictionary.

Just as you would take along your Spanish/English or Russian/English dictionary if you went on a trip to a foreign land, keep your dream dictionary close at hand until you gradually discover you are figuring things out for yourself, based on what the symbols mean to you. And just for fun, before you look up the meaning of a symbol, think about what it means to you. You may be surprised how close you come to the dictionary's definition of the symbol.

When I first began working with dreams, I had one in which one of the symbols was leather. In deciding what leather meant to me, I came up with "thick skin", smells good, strong, natural, and wrinkled (it was an old leather object). And surprise! When I looked it up in "The Dream Book – Symbols For Self-Understanding" by Betty Bethards, one of my favorite books of dream symbols, I discovered I was pretty close. According to that book, leather symbolized toughness, strength and instinctual nature. I hadn't thought about the instinctual nature, but I'll never forget it now!

The meanings of symbols always seemed to stick in my mind better if I tried to figure them out before looking them up, taking into consideration not only what the symbol represents but also how it feels (the texture), what it is used for, where I might find it, its habits (if it's an animal) and basically anything and everything that comes to mind involving that symbol.

When seeing an animal in a dream, consider its life cycle and habits. Is it hatched from an egg (like an idea)? How long does it live? What are its natural enemies? In mulling over all the attributes of the creature, something may "click" about the meaning of the dream. Another thing to consider, with animals, is the meaning of the animal in a deck of medicine cards, which you can get at any New Age store.

Use of dreams to diagnose and treat physical and emotional problems isn't something new. Dreams played an important role in the healing arts of ancient Greece. Even Hippocrates, the father of medicine, studied patients' dreams to come up with advice based on their content. Galen, another early physician (130-200 AD) claimed dreams were necessary for him to diagnose and treat properly. Interestingly, Galen was also among the first physicians to use raw honey in treating wounds and burns. So if you dream of honey and bees you might consider the message of using honey as a treatment for your problem.

Natural honey has healing properties. I first heard about this in 1979 when I wrote an article for the Milwaukee Journal about Dr. T.A. Lanczy, a physician in L'anse, Michigan, who had been treating burns with honey since 1935 and found it preferable to modern medicine. He learned about it in 1934 from a friend who had just finished medical school in Prague and the friend had heard about a Russian method of using honey to treat burns. Dr. Lanczy tried it on a nurse who was badly burned after spilling alcohol onto a flame. He used the traditional method of treating burns which, at the time was petroleum jelly, on one arm and honey on the other. The arm treated with honey did not blister and he discovered that honey was, by far, the better method. So it became Dr. Lanczy's standard treatment for burns. The key, he said, was to cover the wound with honey, sterile gauze and a bandage. The bandage is changed daily for 14 days but the original gauze is left in place with subsequent layers of honey applied over the dressing. To remove the gauze before 14 days will interfere with the healing.

He also used more conventional antibiotics and tetanus shots along with his honey treatment. Honey was effective with frostbite as well – a sweet solution to painful problems.

My honey story may seem like something of a diversion from dreams, but it's not. I mention this to make the dreamer aware of the importance of tuning in to every symbol you can remember from your dream and looking at it just a little closer. If you go to bed at night asking for a dream of healing and you dream of bees and honey, by all means take the time to look into the health benefits of bees and honey. Bee stings, for example, are believed by some to be helpful in the treatment of some forms of arthritis. It's called apitherapy and the bee venom is thought to reduce inflammation.

On the other hand, you might be allergic to bees so seeing a bee in a dream could be a warning.

If dreaming of bowls of gelatin seems to make no sense, don't discard it. Look up gelatin as related to health. A gelatin supplement, high in amino acids, has had a positive effect on joint cartilage, leading to reduced pain and increased range of motion in the knees. Gelatin desserts don't have enough gelatin in them to provide these benefits, but the gelatin desserts in your dreams may just be a clue pointing you in the right direction to the answer to your knee pain. So be open to researching whatever comes up, no matter how unrelated it may appear to the problem at hand.

It is my hope that in the future, traditional medical people will devote more study to dream analysis and working with the patient as a whole. As the medical profession continues to become more open to alternative and complementary healing methods, I'm sure this will happen. But like so many good things, it will take time. And in the meantime, you can be ahead of the curve by letting your dreams be your doctor.

CHAPTER EIGHT

Prescriptions and Advice From the Beyond

Have you ever received a personally significant message from a deceased loved one in a dream and then wondered if the message was really from that person or if it was all your imagination?

Well, the answer is, it could be a little of both. I believe such things do happen. Let's just say I've seen too much evidence that we can receive messages from the beyond, particularly at significant times in our lives when we need to feel the love and guidance of someone who has passed on. But just in case you are more skeptically inclined, let me explain the other view of these situations.

Since we are more likely to accept information from a person we love and trust, our subconscious mind, which affects our dreams, is more likely to present a solution to us in the form of a person or a symbol we know and trust than from someone or something we dislike, distrust or don't know.

For example, suppose you and your Aunt Martha didn't get along. When you were growing up, she was always telling you what to do and how to do it, putting down what you considered great ideas - like how to build a fort or how to make a fishing pole, or what you want to be when you grow up. Perhaps she was the one who told you that you could never be a doctor because you were a girl, or that you couldn't be a professional baseball player because you didn't live in a big city. You get the picture.

On the other hand, suppose you got along very well with your grandmother. Grandma always encouraged your ideas, praised you when you succeeded and urged you to keep on trying when you failed. If you needed help she was there, and if she had a better idea, she suggested it in a way that didn't make you feel like a dumb kid.

If you program your dreams for an answer, it's not likely you're going to pay attention to that answer if Aunt Martha shows up in a dream with some advice. Even if Aunt Martha's advice comes in symbols instead of a direct answer, as it very likely will, you're not likely to even try to figure it out because Aunt Martha never seemed to give a rip about your ideas or problems when she was living, so why would you trust her now that she's dead?

Grandma, on the other hand, was always there for you. Consequently, you are much more likely to heed advice coming from her.

Did Grandma really come to you in a dream? Maybe. Maybe not. The important thing is not whether she really came to you in spirit to help with your problem, but rather, what advice did she have to offer? Whether or not you really saw a ghost is irrelevant. Yes, it may have been Grandma. But it also may have been your all-knowing higher self, providing the answer you already had within yourself, in a form you would accept. You are much more likely to accept information coming from someone you love and trust than from someone who was antagonistic and "know it all."

As I was sitting at my computer this morning, working on this chapter, I was wondering what case studies I might include, since I have a gazillion of them that illustrate situations where dreamers received help from the beyond. But which ones would be the best ones to use?

Then a strange thing happened. Well, maybe not strange for me, since these synchronicities happen all the time, but some folks might consider it strange.

I got a call from a client I'll call Faye. She sounded excited and wanted to know if I was busy, because she had a couple of dreams and really needed to know what they meant. So chapter eight went "on hold" while I took time out to talk to Faye.

As it turned out, this was another of those synchronicities that was meant to happen and I no longer question them. Faye's dreams were a perfect example of how we get answers in dreams from people we love.

First I need to give you a little background. Faye is a beautiful woman in her mid 50s who was an only child. She developed polio when she was six-years-old and as a result her parents, particularly her mother, devoted her life to Faye, making sure she was taken care of, got to school, got the proper rest, etc. She was always there for Faye and mother and daughter had a very close bond.

Faye grew up and married and after her dad died, her mom moved in with Faye and her husband. Eventually her mom's health deteriorated and it became Faye's turn to take care of her mom, which she was happy to do. Finally, at age 90, her mom required so much care she had to go into a nursing home, but Faye visited every day.

When her mom died at age 92, Faye was as heartbroken as if she was 10 years old and lost her mother.

Months and years passed and Faye went on with her life, but her mother was always on her mind.

"I wondered if I'd done the right thing, putting her in a nursing home and allowing her to have medications that sometimes caused her to be confused," Faye said, "but at the same time, I knew I couldn't have taken care of her at home. I felt guilty, but at the same time, I knew I couldn't have done things any differently."

Now – the dream:

In the first dream Faye's husband is asking her if she would like to go for a ride in a buckboard (symbolizing Faye's "rough ride" in life). She says yes and is asked which of three animals she wants to pull her buckboard – a horse (representing strength), a sheep (symbolizing following the crowd) or a snake.

A snake can symbolize different things to different people but after some discussion, we determined that to Faye, who is NOT afraid of snakes in life but was in the dream, the snake symbolized a fear to make changes and move on into a new life.

Because a snake sheds its "old" skin and moves forward with a "new" skin it represented, for Faye, the need to shed her old concerns and move forward.

Next she comes to a building and goes inside to what appears to be a hospital room. Three small boys are in hospital beds. (Small children symbolize ideas, the creative part of the self, and sometimes your own younger self.) In the dream she asks one of the boys what he's doing there and he says, "I can't find my mama." She takes his hand and says, "I know what you mean. I can't find mine either."

He says, "Your mama must be old" and Faye says, "Yes, she is, but I still want my mama."

At that point she wakes up.

The first dream clarified Faye's emotional problem. She'd had a rough life, chose to move forward with strength, but still wanted her mama!

It was the second dream that provided the answer.

In this dream, Faye goes to the nursing home where her mom died and asks where her mom is. She is told they can't find her mother. Faye leaves and drives until she comes to a one-way street a few blocks away, which actually exists, but in the dream, the one-way sign has been turned around.

As she stands there wondering "which way to turn" (which she is actually doing in life, because of her grief over the loss of her mother), she decides to go the way the sign originally pointed – the right (correct) way. And at the end of the street, she finds her mother.

"Mom was young and beautiful and healthy again and she asked what I was doing there," Faye said. "I said, Mom, I'm looking for you."

Her mom smiled and said, "You don't need to look for me anymore. I'm okay."

As much as I have worked with dreams, this was truly an emotional experience and what Faye and I both felt was an answer from her mother that she was okay. She was young, beautiful and healthy again in the afterlife and Faye was free to go on with her life with no feelings of guilt over having done or not done the right thing for her mother. The dream answered her questions.

Another one I'd like to share is from Tiffany, an 18-year-old girl who was dating Brad, a young man the same age, for about two years. Three days after breaking up with Tiffany, Brad dated her friend.

"I was so upset I threw up for three days at the thought of them being together," Tiffany said. "When I saw him again, we fought about it and I told him my friend was a "drama queen" and always did that kind of thing to her friends - like going out with their boyfriends."

Tiffany and Brad made another try at their relationship, but then he went out with another one of her friends. Ultimately Tiffany and Brad broke up, but she still couldn't stop thinking about him and kept asking herself if she should go back to him and maybe it would work.

Then the dream:

Tiffany and Brad are on a huge roller coaster at a local amusement park.

"We were both scared and held hands tightly," Tiffany said. "Everyone is strapped in and the coaster starts but as it begins to go up the slope, it rolls back."

They try again and still it doesn't make it. Finally Tiffany and Brad get off the roller coaster and the maintenance people try again and this time the roller coaster goes right to the top and onward.

"As long as Brad and I were riding that coaster, it wasn't going to make it over the top," Tiffany said. "I woke up realizing Brad and I weren't going to make it and I'm comfortable now with the breakup."

Another client, Maribeth, tells of a dream on the anniversary of her husband, Tim's, diagnosis of cancer that happened on her birthday the previous year. Tim died nine months after that diagnosis. It was the night before her birthday when she had the dream.

"I recalled at bedtime what an awful birthday I'd had the previous year," she said. "I had been widowed three months and still wasn't doing very well. So I went to sleep and asked God to help me have a better birthday than last year. I said it would be different without Tim but I'd appreciate it if it could be a better birthday than that one."

In the dream, Tim called Maribeth on the phone and said "I told her to call you."

Maribeth woke up, saw it was 6 a.m. and realized she'd been dreaming. She closed her eyes to go back to sleep when the phone rang. It was her daughter, calling from Switzerland, to say she knew she was waking Maribeth up but she didn't want her mom to wake up alone without her dad being there.

"All that day I had visits," Maribeth said. Tears brimmed in her eyes as she told the story of the marvelous dream 25 years later.

"I received flowers and phone calls all day," she said. "The very last one was at 10:30 p.m. from my son who was in college. It appeared Tim truly had "told her to call". In fact, he must have told a bunch of people to call!"

It was a birthday Maribeth will never forget.

Yvonne was dating Chuck, a man she met five years after both of them were widowed. Everything about their relationship was running smoothly except one. Chuck still continued to constantly refer to the past, talking about the business he and his wife, Darlene, operated together, trips they enjoyed, dishes she cooked and even her favorite TV shows.

"I was beginning to wonder if he was ever going to come into the present," Yvonne said. "When we were together we really enjoyed each other, but I felt like I was competing with a ghost and I was beginning to wonder if this relationship was worth pursuing."

One particularly stressful night, after Darlene's name had come up again and again, Yvonne went to bed in tears, asking God, the universe and whoever or whatever out there was willing to listen, what she should do.

The answer came from Darlene, in a dream. Yvonne knew it was Darlene because she had seen pictures of her in Chuck's home.

"I still get goose bumps and a lump in my throat when I think about how real and beautiful that dream was," Yvonne said. "In the dream, Darlene, Chuck and I were in a bar, which is a place I seldom go. Darlene pointed to a big hole in Chuck's heart and said to me, "You see where that hole is, in his heart. That's where I used to be. Now it's up to you to fill that hole."

Then Darlene took Yvonne's hand and lovingly placed it in Chuck's and said to him, "Chuck, I was your past. Yvonne is your present and future. And then Darlene walked away with a smile on her face. But before she left, she cautioned Yvonne, saying, "This won't be easy, but believe me, he's worth the wait."

As it turned out, the dream was right. Over the next few weeks and months Chuck began speaking less and less about the past and focusing on the future. Darlene's name still comes up occasionally, as does the name of Yvonne's former husband. But it isn't an everyday occurrence and the couple is moving forward in their new life together.

"I don't know if I would have had the patience to stick with it if it hadn't been for that dream message from Darlene," Yvonne said.

Yvonne never did figure out the significance of the bar scene, since she rarely goes to a bar, but it appears that wasn't important. And you will find this is true. Every single symbol in a dream isn't always significant. Often it's what we refer to as "day residue." The symbol or scene is something nestled in the memory from a recent happening, but it isn't terribly significant to the "answer" in the dream. And the dreamer will know. That "a-ha" feeling is usually your best clue. You get it. If the "a-ha" feeling doesn't happen after awhile when you're trying to figure out the meaning of a symbol, chances are that particular symbol wasn't that important.

These, of course, are all examples of emotional healings and solutions. But dreams work just as well in providing answers to physical problems, with the answers coming from loved ones who have passed on.

Anne has chronic sinusitis. On one particularly bad night she went to bed and asked for an answer to come in her dreams.

In the dream her male cousin (now deceased), with whom she had a very good relationship throughout his life, was arrested for growing marijuana. Since neither Anne nor the cousin had ever used marijuana, this seemed a little strange, but in the dream her cousin tells her there is peppermint growing amidst the marijuana and she should pick it.

Upon awakening, she checked a book on natural remedies to see what peppermint might be used for and found it was suggested as a remedy to clear the sinuses. The recommended method was to put a dab of the peppermint oil on the outside of each nostril.

"That reminded me of another dream I had about cranberries," Anne said. "I was at my deceased grandmother's house. I loved my grandmother and I always enjoyed going there. Her house was always neat and clean but in this dream, I was under the table eating raw cranberries and the house was filthy dirty."

The dirty house symbolized her congested head and constipated body. Suspecting the cranberries might have something to do with her health conditions, she looked them up in the same book on natural healing to find that cranberries contain a form of natural antibiotic. One suggested remedy for sinusitis called for a cup of raw, grated cranberries softened in hot water and sweetened with a little honey.

So you see, strange as it may seem, we do get answers to our problems during the night when we are supposedly "wasting time" sleeping.

While your body is resting your mind is busy processing the events of the day as well as the questions that may have been gnawing at you for months and even years. So it is critical that value in dreams is recognized.

Dreams are anything but meaningless "plays" presented in the mind during the night. They can provide valuable information to help with both physical and emotional problems if we are just willing to make an effort to remember them, jot them down and figure them out.

Personally, I find it pretty entertaining figuring out the answers. Much more fun and practical than crossword puzzles and board games.

CHAPTER NINE

Nightmare Experiences

We often hear the expression that a bad experience "was a nightmare." That is certainly the truth, in more ways than one. The initial experience is a horrifying situation in itself and then bad experiences tend to resurface in our dream life, causing them to linger sometimes for the rest of our lives. Experience like rape and combat are in this category.

The good thing is, by working with those "nightmare" experiences rather than just enduring them, we can turn things around. Nothing will change the fact that we experienced the "nightmare" situation, but by working with the recurring dreams we can learn to deal with it in more productive way.

Deirdre Barrett, assistant professor of psychology in the department of psychiatry at Harvard Medical School, is president of the Association for the Study of Dreams and has a private practice in Cambridge, MA. In editing "Trauma and Dreams," a collection of thoughts and findings on dreams from a number of mental health workers (Barrett, 1996) she recognized the relationship between trauma and dreams in centuries past. Lady Macbeth is one we all remember. While sleepwalking, she dreams of trying to wash the blood of her murder victim from her hands.

William Shakespeare wasn't into analyzing dreams. He was just out to write a good story and "Macbeth" was one of his best.

If Lady Macbeth were sitting in my office today, sharing her dream of trying to wash the blood from her hands, I would have some advice for her. But first, you need to forget that there was a murder involved, because, as a psychotherapist, the rules of client confidentiality would not apply here. Psychotherapists are obligated to inform authorities of any situation in which a person is a threat to him/herself or others and certainly murder would fall into that category!

So let's just assume that Lady Macbeth was involved in a terrible accident in which someone was killed and she's feeling guilty. Today, we call it PTSD – post-traumatic stress disorder. By working with her dreams, she could alleviate some of the stress and perhaps even resolve the situation in her own mind.

Hypnosis is often helpful in inducing dreams when a person actually wants to work with a troubling dream. To do this, I would recommend working with a trained hypnotherapist at least two or three times, to induce relaxation and give you the suggestion that the next time you are having this troubling dream you will immediately become aware of it and be able to interact with the symbols. Rather than running from a frightening attacker or scene, for example, you will turn and face the threatening situation and ask who it is or what it wants from you.

After two or three sessions with a professional hypnotherapist, you should be able to induce this relaxed state yourself and give yourself the suggestion that you become aware when you are dreaming and be able to control the action in that dream. It's called lucid dreaming. Lucid dreams generally occur closer to morning. You may already have experienced them. In this state, the dreamer is aware he is dreaming but remains asleep. But what you may not have known is that you can be the director as well as the actor in these kinds of dreams and you can change the action by confronting the frightening figure or situation and asking whatever questions you want to ask.

Here is an example of how we can direct our dreams in the lucid dreaming state, taken from a dream told to me, in conversation, by a man who knew about my work with dreams. Let's call him Henry. In the dream, Henry was in Africa and he had foolishly decided to hike down a dirt road to a small town where he wanted to purchase a drinking glass (yes dreams are strange). Perhaps he was "thirsting" for something, like knowledge.

Although he knew there was a pride of lions in the vicinity, all he had to defend himself with was a little stick. Halfway to his destination he looked behind him and saw that the pride of lions had gathered on the road. But more alarming yet, a huge male lion was loping down the road after him. He wondered if he could defend himself with the little stick.

Now, in dreams of this sort, in the face of such a frightening situation, we usually wake up, but Henry was able to direct his dream. Suddenly he remembered that he had a pistol stuck in his belt, but he also know there were laws against shooting wildlife without a permit. What to do?

He decided his life was more important, the laws be damned. However, there was still a problem. Would his aim be accurate and would the bullet stop the lion? At this point he awakened.

These kinds of dreams are often repetitive and the dreamer, over time, is able to resolve the situation by taking some symbolic action which results in a resolution in the waking life.

This is kind of one of those "which comes first – the chicken or the egg" situations, since solving the problem on the waking level will also transfer to the dream. In Henry's dream, the lion might have eventually morphed into a house cat, for example, once the problem was solved on the waking level.

Had Henry actually been a client and had time to discuss his dream I would have told him my impression of it. He was trying to make a major decision of some kind in his waking life that involved risks. He didn't know which way to turn, but my guess would be, at that point in his life he had decided to take the risk.

Since Henry was already skilled at lucid dreaming and was able to direct his dreams, I would have suggested that he program his dreams the next night to discover he had a magical type of gun that would paralyze the lion so it could not run. Then Henry could approach the lion and engage him in conversation, asking "why are you chasing me?" (Remember this is a dream and you can do anything in a dream.)

Alternatively, Henry could have a magical gun that hits the target simply by the dreamer willing where the bullet should go, but then the "lion" would not have been able to provide the needed information about why he was chasing Henry.

Once you realize you are having a lucid dream, it is much better to face the fearful object and ask what it is trying to tell you than to destroy it. By destroying the symbol, you still have the unanswered question – what was that all about?

There are also books on self-hypnosis that can help you access this state of lucid dreaming. (More on that later.) And yes, you can learn to do self-hypnosis easily and it is safe. I taught myself when I was 7 years old because I was afraid of the dentist. That dentist had the breath of a buffalo and his office, on the third floor of an old, dark and dreary apartment building, was nothing short of a chamber of horrors. In those days (the 1940s and '50s) nothing was used to deaden pain except for an extraction. To avoid the horrible sound of that drill, the buffalo breath and the trauma and drama going on in my mouth, I would imagine myself swimming in Ice Lake which was just down the hill from our house in Iron River in the Upper Peninsula of Michigan. I loved swimming and still do, so the minute I sat in that chair overlooking main street I'd imagine myself in one of the cars that was going by and getting a ride back home and escaping from the dentist's chair and then I would go through all the motions, in my mind, of going swimming. I'd see myself putting on my bathing suit, feel my feet against the warm blacktop road as I walked down the hill to the lake, feel the cool, wet sand oozing up between my toes, the sudden slap of the cold water as I ran into the lake and then floating on my back, watching the clouds and birds overhead. I didn't know what I was doing was actually called self-hypnosis until years later, as an adult. But the point I'm making here is it's easy and safe. After all, I did learn it when I was 7 and I figured it out for myself.

Just as I used self-hypnosis to "escape" the dentist's chair, I have also used it (and you can, too) to make myself aware that I was in a lucid dream, confront the scary figures and work with them.

Working with lucid dreams is nothing new. As early as the eighth century AD, Tibetan Buddhists pursued the cultivation of dream lucidity and achieving mastery of lucid dreams was considered a prerequisite to seeking enlightenment.

Islam also encouraged followers to train themselves in the skills of lucid dreaming. ("Our Dreaming Mind", Robert L. Van de Castle, Ph.D., 1994)

So if Lady Macbeth were sitting across from me today, as a hypnotherapist, I would induce her into a relaxed stage, take her into the troubling dream, and have her work with it, perhaps asking herself what it was about the accident (remember, it can't be a murder in this situation) that made her feel responsible. Even if she actually was at fault, she could process her feelings in the dream and acknowledge that she did not intend for it to happen and it was, indeed, an accident.

She might visit, in the hypnotic state and later in her dreams, with the person who died in that accident and explain to that person how it happened and how she feels about causing the pain and loss for that person and his/her family.

After she visits with the victim of the accident, I might have Lady Macbeth take a minute, in the hypnotic state, to listen to anything that person has to say to her. Often, the person a client feels he/she has "wronged" will respond with a message of forgiveness and understanding that puts the client at ease for the first time in years.

After going through a couple of sessions of hypnotherapy to show Lady Macbeth how to induce a lucid dream and work with it, she would be able to induce this relaxed state herself and continue to work with her feelings on her own.

I would probably leave her with the post-hypnotic suggestion that when she was ready to let the guilt and bad feelings go for good, then she could wash the blood from her hands, watch it go down the drain until every trace of it was gone and become aware that her hands were clean – an excellent symbol that she has washed away the guilt and resolved her feelings.

Of course, the answer doesn't always come on the first try and it isn't always that simplistic. In hypnosis, as in dreams, you just never know what is going to come up, but the one sure thing is whatever does come up, you can work with it, provided you are willing to take the time. Because it's all coming from your subconscious, it is unique to you.

The classic example of dealing with a lucid dream is for the dreamer to stop running away and confront the object that is terrorizing her, asking what it means.

Sometimes the answer comes right away and is pretty direct. "I'm your boss and I'm going to fire you if you don't learn that new computer program by Wednesday."

Other times it's not that easy. The answer may come in a symbol or a statement that seems to be a riddle or the nightmare figure continues to attempt to intimidate and terrorize the dreamer. At this point the dreamer might instruct herself to rise above the scene and from a perch where she is out of danger, demand an answer.

Having the dreamer confront and slay the dream "dragon" is not recommended because then the question of "why are you bothering me" won't be answered and the dragon of your dreams will never be truly "slain."

Practice makes perfect. And with continued practice, working with lucid dreams becomes easier and even fun.

Nora, one of the participants in my dissertation on using dreams to diagnose and treat physical and emotional problems, was 55 years old and suffered with health problems including obesity, diabetes, asthma, allergies, marital and job stress. Of the eight dreams she shared, one recurring dream was particularly significant. During her six pregnancies and one miscarriage, Nora had been chased by a man with a pumpkin head dressed in a silver suit. She would try to hide in an alley near her mother's home, which she was very familiar with and she felt safe there. The pumpkin headed man never caught up with her but she would always wake up feeling exhausted. After the pregnancy was over, she wouldn't have the dream until she became pregnant again. Since she stopped having children she has never had the dream.

In analyzing the dream years later, Nora felt the pumpkin headed man may have symbolized a penis and her concerns about getting pregnant and wanting to escape from it.

"Had I known about lucid dreaming back then, I could have turned around and asked the pumpkin man who he was and what the hell he wanted," Nora said. "I would have saved myself a lot of stress and gotten a good night's sleep."

CHAPTER TEN

When Being "Asleep" is Being More Alert

Let me say, before you begin reading this chapter, that self-hypnosis is definitely NOT necessary to work with your dreams. It's just another tool to enhance your skills. You can work with spontaneous dreams just as easily. The advantages of self-hypnosis are two. First, it provides a wonderful feeling of relaxation, and second, it helps you program your dreams to get the answers you are seeking.

Lest you worry about self-hypnosis being dangerous, be aware that ALL hypnosis is actually self-hypnosis. Rather than being "asleep," hypnosis is a relaxed state in which your subconscious is actually more alert and aware of the suggestions you are giving to yourself. In any situation where a person agrees to be induced into a hypnotic trance, that person is totally in charge. It's not like the old movies (and even some newer ones!) where the villain is an evil hypnotist who has the "victim" under his complete control. That applies to self- hypnosis as well as to hypnosis induced by a professional hypnotherapist. You are in control. You are simply in a relaxed state in which your subconscious mind is open to the suggestions you or a professional hypnotherapist are giving it.

Yes – I know about stage hypnotists who get people to act like a drunk or quack like a duck. Two types of people attend stage hypnosis shows. The first group is those who want to be hypnotized for an excuse to have a little fun and be the center of attention for a while, and there's nothing wrong with that. It's all in good fun. The other group is those who want to prove they can't be hypnotized, and usually they won't be. They'll just enjoy the show.

There is a big difference between hypnosis and hypnotherapy. Hypnosis is primarily entertainment. Hypnotherapy involves using the hypnotic state to accomplish a therapeutic purpose such as solving a problem or recovering a memory.

Even under hypnosis, recovered memories may not be accurate. However, they are always something the individual can work with because whatever comes up is unique to that person. Is it imagination? Maybe. But whatever you imagine is unique to you, so it means something to you personally.

As a past life regression therapist, I suspect that sometimes memories that surface under hypnosis may be "true", but they actually happened in another lifetime. For example, in cases of child abuse which are remembered in later years, a person may remember his/her father as being the abuser when, in truth, it was the father in another lifetime. Or the present-day father may have been a brother in another lifetime and the brother was the "doer of the deed" in that other lifetime. It gets a little complicated. But the thing to be aware of is "recovered memories" should always be given the benefit of a doubt, especially in situations involving crimes or serious accusations that could affect another person's life.

The same can apply to dreams, where the dreamer sees a specific person committing an action. It's possible the person the dreamer "sees" may actually be someone who committed a particular act (maybe it was just a kid taking something out of the cookie jar). But it could be something from a past life OR, more likely, the person the dreamer sees may be a symbol of some characteristic the dreamer himself possesses that he/she sees in the dream figure. If the dreamer sees a favorite teacher writing a message on the blackboard, it may very well be the message is coming to the dreamer in a form he/she is willing to accept. If the dreamer thinks her cousin Harriet is a jealous, meddling bitch, then seeing Harriet in a dream may indicate the dreamer has similar characteristics herself but is not quite willing to recognize them. (Harriet, being a female figure, would be a subconscious aspect of the self.)

In a past life dream, for example, a dreamer might recall her mother leaving her alone at home when she was an infant. It's possible the mother in the dream may even actually be the dreamer's mother today, but in this life that mother would never dream (no pun intended) of leaving an infant home alone. The dream might very well explain, though, why the dreamer doesn't quite trust her mother today and has no real reason (at least none she knows about) to feel that way.

One clue to remember in determining if a dream is a past life dream is to notice the clothing worn by the people in the dreams and the backgrounds. In a past life dream the people will be wearing clothes from an earlier time period and the buildings and transportation will be from another era.

The important thing about a past life dream, particularly traumatic ones, is to understand that past life is over. The lesson was learned in that life and there is no reason to carry it forward.

Peggy, now in her 40s, was married and the mother of two grown children but she still had feelings for her first love, Tom. When she and Tom were dating something always seemed to get in the way of their being together. Another thing she found unusual was that Tom had never made any sexual advances toward her. A dream provided the answer.

In this dream, Peggy was walking alongside a curtain, like one you'd find on a stage in a theater. She was a nun. On the other side of the curtain she could see the shoes of a man keeping in step with her. When they reached the end of the curtain, Peggy looked up and to her amazement discovered the man keeping in step with her was Tom and he was a priest.

"Whether the dream was true or symbolic, that explained why we never got together in this lifetime," Peggy said. "We both would have taken a vow of chastity."

When experiencing a traumatic dream like this one, become aware of the feelings you had in the dream and ask yourself when you have experienced those feelings in this life. Through working with the symbols and the feelings we often see a pattern emerge.

For example, in this life you may resent your husband or wife "abandoning you" by going out and doing something on his/her own and leaving you behind. That feeling of rejection may have originated in another lifetime, when you were left alone, as a helpless infant.

Just be willing to look at all the aspects of the dream, especially the feelings, if, on awakening, they still seem real. Jot down immediately the characters, symbols and feelings so you can work with them later. Just taking the time to think about all these aspects of a dream will provide some insight into situations you may be dealing with in your life today that originated in another lifetime.

I've digressed here a bit, I know, but the information about past lives, I feel, is important to anyone working with self-hypnosis and dreams. It's also a very good reason for the amateur to NEVER attempt to hypnotize anyone else. You can safely work with yourself to program your dreams and you will always "wake up" because even if you should fall asleep, it will just be a natural, relaxing sleep. However, only a professional hypnotherapist should work with another person. The amateur, for example, won't know what to do if his/her subject suddenly begins speaking a foreign language or finds himself in a traumatic situation, such as being burned at the stake.

This isn't going to happen under self-hypnosis because you are the "director" of this production.

So now we are ready to attempt self-hypnosis.

First of all, be aware that "sleep" is a misnomer for hypnosis. Rather than sleep, hypnosis is a state of heightened awareness. The body is totally relaxed leaving the mind free to focus on other things, and more specifically, whatever the situation is that you want to work on. You will be aware of outside sounds. You just won't care about them. But should any emergency occur when you are in this relaxed state (like the baby waking up from her nap or the house catching fire) you will be immediately aware and able to respond appropriately.

It's best, however, to set aside a time and place where you can reasonably expect an emergency will NOT occur. For example, make sure someone else is in the house in case the baby does wake up. Being a mom myself, I know how difficult it is to focus on anything when there are children in the house, even if they are sleeping.

Turn the telephone off and select a room you can darken somewhat (or do this at night). Select a relaxing New Age type CD or tape (one that doesn't have a rhythm or vocals that will distract you) and pick the most comfortable chair in the house. You can also use your bed, but a chair is better because you are less likely to fall asleep.

You can "talk to yourself" in your head as you do this, or you may want to make a tape recording of this script or something similar – whatever suits your purpose. The exact words aren't important. This is just a guide.

Either way, talking to yourself in your head or on a tape, take time to picture each step and feel the progressive relaxation as you move through the script. This focusing will allow you to "zone out" so your subconscious mind can accept suggestions for the dream information you want to receive.

All settled in your chair now, in semi-darkness, New Age music playing softly; you're ready to begin.

Take a nice deep breath, lean back in your chair and relax as you gently close your eyes, taking time to feel the surface of the chair against your body and letting your body melt into the chair.

Take another nice deep breath, and as you release that breath, release all the cares of your day, all the cares of your life. For now, just let them float away as you focus on the feeling and the sound of your breath, coming in and going out.

Feel yourself breathing in calmness, peace and relaxation and breathing out any stress or tension you may be holding.

Now relax your scalp and forehead. Feel the skin of your scalp and your forehead just melting, smoothing.

Now relax the muscles around your eyes and then around your mouth and jaw. And for a second, just pay attention to how that feels. Let your mouth open slightly, if that's comfortable for you.

Now imagine yourself in a warm, relaxing hot tub. And as you relax in that hot tub, feel your toes relaxing and then your heels and your ankles, your knees, your thighs, your hips. Feel yourself melting into the chair. And as you relax you can feel that warm relaxed, melting feeling moving up your spine, one vertebra at a time, until it reaches your neck and scalp.

Now picture yourself at the top of a staircase. This can be any staircase you want it to be – a real one you remember or an imaginary one that appeals to you. Just pick out something you like. (I often imagine the stairs that went from my grandma's apartment upstairs to our apartment on the first floor in my early years. It was a good time with a lot of happy memories and I also considered my grandmother a very wise woman and a person I could trust.)

At the top of the stairs, picture 10 steps as you begin moving down, deeper and deeper into relaxation, deeper with every breath, imagining the feeling as each foot sets down on the stairs, noting the texture of the stairs if you choose to be barefoot. Maybe it's cool marble or warm wood. You get the picture. Just let your imagination run wild.

10 – Say the number, picture the number in your mind, and then erase it as you go deeper.

9 – Erase the nine now.

8 – Going deeper still.

7 –

6 – More and more relaxed.

5 – Deeper and deeper relaxed as you prepare to request a dream that will provide an answer to your question about (your asthma, your relationship, whatever...).

4-

3 – Any outside sounds you hear are just sounds, so you can just let them go. But should any emergency occur while you are in this relaxed state, you will recognize it immediately and become fully alert.

2 – Focus your attention on the tip of your nose now. See the tip of your nose. Anytime your thoughts wander, just bring your focus back there, to the tip of your nose.

1 – Ready now to ask your subconscious for a dream that will provide some information about your problem.

Imagine now, that you are walking on a beach. It's a beautiful, warm, sandy beach and you can hear the waves against the shore and feel the coolness of the sand under your feet where the water has soaked into it.

You're all alone and enjoying this beautiful day as you continue to walk alone, feeling the sun on your shoulders, feeling the breeze against your skin.

Up ahead you see someone in a lawn chair. You wonder who it is, and as you get closer and closer the figure begins to look familiar.

Take your time getting there, enjoying the day, the sounds of the seagulls, the sound of the wind in the trees, any sounds or sights you might enjoy in this place. Maybe even imagine you are picking a flower or a seashell as you walk along.

Finally you reach the figure in the lawn chair. He/she smiles and greets you. And you recognize this figure as your higher self – the part of you that knows everything about you, the part of you that knows the answers.

So you sit down and tell your higher self what it is you would like to know, and why it is important to you. You ask your higher self to send you that information in a dream.

Then, when you are ready, you can thank your higher self for listening, turn and walk back down the beach, until once again, you come back to your staircase and begin your way back to the present, knowing that you have left the suggestion for an informative dream with your higher self and you're ready to accept that information when it comes.

1 – Taking a nice deep relaxing breath now as you begin to return to the present.

2 –

3 – Feeling good about yourself and what you accomplished.

4 – Feeling your energy return.

5 – Moving your fingers and toes around a little.

6 – Connecting back to your chair, your room and your surroundings.

7 –

8 –

9 – Returning with peace, confidence and empowerment, knowing you are ready to accept any information your subconscious may provide regarding your problem.

10 – Wide awake now, whenever you are ready.

Now wasn't that easy? And relaxing?

Now all you need to do is wait for the dream information to come through. For that reason, the closer to bedtime you can do this, the better it will be. Also be aware that you may get information from sources other than your dreams. Once your subconscious has focused on providing you with answers, you are more "tuned in" to information that may come from other sources as well. You may be driving along and hear something on the radio or stop for lunch in a restaurant and overhear a conversation that is the perfect answer to your problem. Or a friend may give you the name of a great doctor who has helped her with the same health problem you have. Just be open to whatever information comes your way.

CHAPTER ELEVEN

Imagination is Important

Using dreams to solve life's problems isn't some "New Age" idea that just evolved over the past few years. On the contrary, it's another of those ancient practices that has been resurrected from the past and like many "new" and "alternative" healing practices that have been rediscovered, it has been put down by the conventional, scientifically minded folks as New Age nonsense. Much of dream analysis hasn't been scientifically proven, but it has been around for thousands of years and it has worked. History tells us that.

I've already mentioned Hippocrates and Galen. But there are others who relied on dreams as valued sources of information. In theuric medicine, practiced in Aesculapian temples (370 BC), patients described stories from dreams that had a healing effect on their bodies.

Aesculapius is believed to have been an actual healer during that time, although he was later deified (Van de Castle) and dubbed the son of Apollo. But whether Aesculpiuis was real or not isn't the issue. What is true is that the temples did exist and people came to them to request dreams to help them with their physical problems.

"What has happened to this tradition?" Meredith Sabini, Ph.D., asks. "Are there any aspects of it that could be resurrected and integrated into today's healing arts?"

Sabini did a study in an attempt to answer these questions, using a collection of 60 dreams specifically related to general and psychosomatic illnesses. She found that dreams not only address illness, but also bring to light crucial factors that could affect treatment, such as the unconscious need for symptoms, functions of symptoms and sometimes unconscious resistance to treatment.

For example, a dream might alert an individual as to why he might "need" a particular ailment. Let's say the person has asthma. (And this is definitely not saying the person is faking his/her illness. It's a real thing.) What that person might not realize on a conscious level is that his asthma benefits him in some way. Perhaps it enables that person to avoid being around animals.

Why would a person want to avoid animals? It may not be as simple as wanting to get out of cleaning the barn or the litter box!

Symbols in dreams and in hypnotherapy are often very similar, so I will relate to a past life regression experience from when I was first introduced to past life regression therapy in the early 1980s by Dr. Barbara Young, a transpersonal psychotherapist. I didn't "believe in" past lives at the time. Having been raised Catholic I was taught that we have one life only and we'd better get it right or we would burn forever in Hell. But reincarnation has actually been a part of all religions at some time. Some have just chosen to eliminate it.

Brian Weiss, M.D. one of the most famous past life regressionists, in his book, "Through Time Into Healing," (Simon and Schuster, 1992) notes that in his research into the history of Christianity he discovered early references to reincarnation in the New Testament were deleted in the fourth century by the Emperor Constantine when Christianity became the official religion of the Roman Empire.

Apparently Constantine did not want people to think they had another chance at getting things right.

Dr. Young just "happened" to be traveling through town and was teaching some workshops on regression and dream work.

Now we know nothing ever just "happens" by accident. There is that thing called synchronicity, when things happen because they are meant to happen, and at that point in my life it was time for me to be introduced to the interests that would ultimately become my life's work.

I was in my early 40s then and no "spring chicken," but often midlife is the time when our focus begins to shift, sending us off in directions we may never have considered in our younger years. I have since come to believe that past lives aren't something to be "believed in." They simply ARE. Like gravity, they are there and it doesn't matter if you believe in them or not.

In this particular case, a past life regression called attention to my reason for being severely allergic to cats.

As an objective newspaper reporter and a Catholic, I totally disbelieved in past lives, but I decided a story about Dr. Young and her work might make an interesting article. Besides, it might prove useful in my fiction writing. So I agreed to a past life regression to find out why I was so allergic to cats.

I went into a trance easily. No surprise there since even though I lacked formal training at that point in time, I had been using self-hypnosis since I was 7 years old. Expecting to experience nothing, I was amazed to see myself as a young man in sandals standing in an arena. Off to my right I could see lions, waiting for their afternoon snack – me! I was not aware of what I might have done to become lion food, but having attended a Catholic school back in the 1940s and '50s, my first thought was that I was a Christian being fed to the cats.

Oh yawn! I thought. The lions (big cats) are going to have me for lunch and that's why I'm allergic to cats. Big deal. I could have made that story up myself!

As it turned out, that wasn't even close.

The lion was released, came into the arena and then hunkered down at my feet, looking up at me with those beautiful big brown eyes. I reached down and patted his head, noticing the huge paws with their sharp claws that were supposed to turn me into mincemeat. But the lion didn't move.

The soldiers began to stab the lion for not doing it's job (killing me) and I began sobbing (in reality). At that point I went into an asthma attack.

Discussing this with Dr. Young later, I realized my allergy to cats stemmed from such a deep affection for the animals that I could not bear to be around them because of my dread of losing them.

Whether I actually lived that life or if it was symbolic, I don't know. Initially it made no sense, but as often happens with past life regressions, the truth reveals itself over days, weeks and even months. I realized the problem with caring too much about animals weeks later when we had to euthanize one of our two beloved Basset hounds. As my husband was taking the dog to the veterinarian I went into an asthma attack just like in the "past life" when I couldn't deal with the sight of the lion being stabbed to death.

It was at that point that the truth came through, almost like a voice. If I was going to have an animal, unless I chose a tortoise, I was going to outlive the pet so I had better get used to having to let it go.

Until then I had been able to be around a cat only about 20 minutes before having serious breathing problems. (Dogs, rabbits and other furry critters were less of a problem, but still a danger.) After the realization about the meaning of the past life regression, I was able to be around a cat for up to an hour and a half before beginning to have a mild reaction. The regression provided the insight I needed to deal with my allergies and asthma. It wasn't a cure but it was definitely helpful.

The same type of thing can happen with a dream, since dreams and hypnotic regressions are very similar. Often, just like in a dream, the symbols that come up in a regression are not direct answers as one might expect, but symbolic clues. It's up to the dreamer/detective to put the clues together and solve the mystery. So while this particular experience involving my allergy to cats wasn't actually a dream, it could have been and it's a perfect example of how information from a dream can shed light on the reasons for the unconscious need for symptoms. In this case, I needed my allergy to cats to prevent me from becoming emotionally attached to them. On a subconscious level, I didn't want to deal with the trauma of ever losing a beloved cat again.

A dream might also reveal unconscious resistance to treatment. Having arthritis, for example, might be painful and debilitating but it can also bring the victim a lot of sympathy and attention. Special accommodations may be needed for this person. On a conscious level, the person would "do anything" to be normal, but on an unconscious level the illness is bringing the person attention he/she would never have without the "unwanted" health problem. The arthritis has become his identity; consequently, there may be subconscious resistance to treatment and cure.

And again, I stress this is NOT to say a person is creating his/her own illness for attention. Statements like that make me furious and I hear them all the time in New Age circles. Sometimes, I think, we simply have what we have and our challenge in life is to work at it. Maybe it's karma. Maybe it's something else. But the best we can do is make do with what we have and work to improve. Getting back to "normal" may never happen, but we learn in the process of trying, and dreams can help with this.

Pathognomic dreams (from the Greek word meaning "to know") are dreams in which people experience symptoms that manifest in their waking life.

Menstruation, while not a disease, is a physical condition that often brings up graphic imagery in dreams. Women about to menstruate or actually having a period often report having bloody, gory dreams. Bloody imagery is also often present with an impending miscarriage. A. Ziegler, in a 1980 paper on heart failure and aporetic (doubting) dreams, observed that certain kinds of traumatic dreams preceded heart failure. (I could find no further information on specifically what kind of dreams these were.)

Therapists who use dreams in working with patients have found that by tracking their dreams from the beginning of treatment, they can monitor the patient's progress or lack of it. Examples of some positive symbols are ripening fruit, healthy plants and buildings under construction. Symbols that indicate a need to program dreams in a positive direction include withering plants, dark and dreary weather, muddy water and vehicles with flat tires or broken parts.

One patient, prior to having a flare-up with sciatica, dreamed of being in a basement with rusting, damaged pipes and broken stairs. The bottom level of the house, in this case, related to the lower portion of the body – the legs and feet. Other times, however, the basement might relate to the unconscious. It's back to that old "a-ha" factor again. If you find yourself in a basement in your dreams, some self examination will tell you if you're having problems or potential problems with the lower limbs and feet or if something in your subconscious is trying to surface.

Which brings me to sex in dreams. When trying to bring something to a conscious level, people often experience dreams of marriage, sex, signing a contract or other forms of getting together in a dream. Usually this represents the unconscious (represented by a female figure) uniting with the conscious (a male figure) to bring the unconscious information to awareness.

Wedding and sex dreams often occur just before a person becomes consciously aware of a forgotten memory, an idea or virtually anything the dreamer has not been consciously aware of.

Unfortunately, dream answers don't usually manifest in a "flash of light." More often, it involves working with a dream journal over a period of time, monitoring the symbols and noting how they change over time. For example, a dreamer might initially be trying to drive an old car, but the tires are flat and he can't see through the dirty windshield. Initially the dreamer may not even be the driver, indicating that in his waking state he feels like he's not "in the driver's seat." Someone else – a boss or a spouse – is calling the shots.

As healing takes place, over time, the dream changes. The tires are no longer flat but they may be low, the car won't go very fast and the windshield wipers aren't quite doing their job, but at least the dream driver can see through the windshield. In the end, the car is running smoothly, the dreamer is in the driver's seat and can see the road ahead.

The dream, in this case, is one of those nagging repetitive dreams that keep trying to give you a message, so make note of even the slightest changes in a repetitive dream in your journal. As things improve on the waking level, the dream monitors the physical/emotional situation so it also becomes a progress report.

With a dream of this type, the dreamer can actually encourage healing by programming a change in the dream content. This is kind of working in reverse. Instead of programming oneself for physical healing, you might program yourself to dream of a new car, in good condition. You see, dreams work both ways. Improvement in the dream leads to improvement in waking life and improvement in a physical and emotional problem in waking life results in more positive dreams.

In a 1975 article in the "National Enquirer," Vasily Kasatkin, a psychiatrist at the Leningrad Neurosurgical Institute, noticed that dreams of body wounds were among the most serious indications of illness before the illness was actually diagnosed by traditional means. Dreams of being shot in the heart, stabbed in the back or drowning may be the precursor to physical or emotional problems and may occur anywhere from a couple of weeks to a year before a traditional diagnosis. Again, intuition plays a huge part in determining what your own dream symbols mean. Being stabbed in the heart could indicate a potential heart problem or it might indicate the feeling that one is about to be "stabbed in the heart" or "stabbed in the back" emotionally by a trusted friend.

In the case of wounds, pay attention to who is doing the wounding. It may be that you are having a problem with that actual person in your waking life but it could also indicate if you are aware of the problem on a conscious level. If a male person is inflicting the injury you are probably consciously aware of the fact that something is wrong – that you are "heartbroken" or someone is giving you a "pain in the neck." And it may be the person in your dream. And since everyone in a dream USUALLY represents the dreamer him/herself, be aware that the person inflicting your would could be yourself. You are "bringing it on yourself."

If the person inflicting the injury is female (unconscious aspect of yourself), pay special attention because it may indicate a problem is developing in that area of the body but you are not yet consciously aware of it.

Kasatikin said dreams are sentries that watch over our health. There are nerves coming to the brain from every part of the body and they relay signals of impending illness that the subconscious translates into dreams. Charlene's abscessed tooth, mentioned in an earlier chapter, is a good example of this. Her dream was telling her she had an infection in her body before she actually became aware of it.

H.A. Wilmer, in writing of war dreams of Vietnam veterans, tells of a patient who realized his greatest fear was within himself (Barrett, 1996). Initially the veteran, in his dream, heard a grenade outside. In a later dream, he heard a roaring lion outside. Finally he saw himself reflected in the window as he closed it to keep the lion out. It was then he realized he was facing his problem. The problem could be seen within himself (as indicated in his reflection in the window) rather than from outside sources represented by the grenade and the lion.

All of this may sound like it requires a considerable stretch of the imagination to work with dreams and the truth is, it does. Everything starts with imagination. Every book, every song, every painting, even every building, starts with someone's imagination.

I have a banner in my office that says, "Imagination is more important than knowledge. Knowledge is limited. Imagination encircles the world." – Albert Einstein.

Now Albert Einstein was a pretty smart guy, so I don't doubt what he said in the least.

In modern society, for the last century, we have been taught to disregard imagination in favor of scientifically provable hard facts gathered by medical devices showing tracings on screens or images in photographs.

I can remember back in my grade school days being told my "head was in the clouds" and that all I wanted to do was be on the "silver screen". I had NO desire to be on the silver screen, or any place where I would be the center of attention, for that matter. I was actually a pretty shy kid. But I must admit, I was always imagining stories in my mind and that was a quality the "good sisters" in St. Agnes School certainly did not appreciate. My poor parents were constantly being told I didn't apply myself. Creativity was considered worthless daydreaming.

Imagination, while it can't be measured and dissected, is critical in solving problems. So in working with dreams, be open to working with imagination. Imagine what a symbol means to you. Think on it and just let your mind wander and jot down whatever comes up. And don't forget my "Balloon Method" mentioned earlier (on page 14.)

Now that you are ready to start working with your own dreams, here is a quick list of things to do and remember as you begin this fascinating journey into the discoveries that can occur during that one-third of your life you spend in bed when, until now, you thought you were totally oblivious to the world around you.

1. Immediately upon awakening write down the dream. Write single word descriptions first and go back to fill in once your list is complete.
2. Make note of symbols, colors, people, sounds, settings, costumes, etc. In short, list everything you can remember. A good way to do this is to list the symbols, feelings, etc. on the left side of a sheet of paper, like a spelling list and then directly across from the symbol, list what it means to you. Often, by the time you have finished, a pattern will have emerged.
3. Dreams may not have a "story line," but the symbols and patterns tell a story all the same.
4. When writing your dream in a journal, give it a date and a title and note if anything was bothering you, physically or emotionally, at that time. If, in the future, physical or emotional problems become recognizable on a conscious

level, the title and date will enable you to look back and see when the message began to come through. This is important, not so much for that particular problem, but in alerting you as to how far ahead your dreams may begin to reveal future concerns.

An example of the title and date is this dream I randomly picked from my journal of 12 year's worth of dreams. I call it "Golden Wedding" and it was dated December 26, 2001.

In the dream I am marrying a man who, in real life, is just an acquaintance. He's someone I consider intelligent, outspoken and relatively well off financially. The decision to marry this man, in the dream, is a sudden one and we decide on 3 p.m. I have a long gold satin dress and I order a small wreath of flowers to wear as a veil. The entire dream involves preparations for the wedding but we never actually get to the ceremony.

I don't always write out my analysis. I leave it up to you whether you want to do that or not. Most of the time, after reading through the symbols and what they mean to you, the message in the dream becomes clear and you may or may not choose to write it out.

This dream obviously had something to do with striving for wealth since I was wearing the gold dress and the man in the dream was someone I saw as financially successful. Chances are, at that time I may have had an inspiration for a story or article, which would bring me financial gain, but it was still in the "incubation" stage. This would be the reason for the wedding – to bring the inspiration to the conscious level. My unconscious desire was about to unite with my conscious self (represented by a male person – the financially successful man.). The 3 p.m. wedding prompted me to look up the number three in numerology which, in my favorite dream symbol book by Betty Bethards, indicates the trinity of mind, body, spirit harmony. The number three indicates a spiritual message but it could have other implications as well. What occurred to me immediately is the 3 o'clock coffee break — time to take a break. So I guess it was time for me to take a break and work on whatever was inspiring me at that particular time.

Again, we're back to what does a symbol mean for you?

Since this particular dream was all about preparing for a wedding (uniting my subconscious to the conscious) and the wedding never happened in the dream, it was something I could look back on later as a starting point, where an idea that would produce financial gain began to manifest. But first, as the dream indicated, I had to become more self assured and outspoken (like the personality of the man in my dream).

CHAPTER TWELVE

Even Scary Dreams Can Be Helpful

So far I've mentioned mostly ancient uses of dreams in problem solving, taking us back to Grecian temples, exotic tribal cultures and Native American practices most Americans really aren't familiar with. But dream work in problem solving has also been and continues to be used in modern times. In the early 20th century, before the term "New Age" was coined in reference to pretty much anything that wasn't standard medical procedure, Edgar Cayce, sometimes called "The Sleeping Prophet," would put himself into a trance and give readings, which provided information for individuals seeking healings. While in trance, he was in a dreamlike state and many of his readings related to dreams. Cayce, who died in 1945, was neither a medical person nor a "New Age" person, but he had this gift for providing information on healing and 14,879 of those readings ("The Edgar Cayce Remedies", Wm. A. McGarey, M.D., Bantam Books, 1983) still exist and are recorded in the library of the Association for Research and Enlightenment in Virginia Beach, Va.

    A.R.E. is an educational and research organization devoted to disseminating Cayce's views on dreams and other topics. ("Our

Dreaming Mind", Robert L. Van DeCastle, Ph.D., Ballantine Books, 1994.)

As a Christian, Cayce was upset about his gift in the beginning and with good reason. During the dark ages, the Christian church opposed dream analysis, believing it to be magic. This was because of a mistranslation of the Bible by St. Jerome, who had an interesting experience with dreams himself and was apparently frightened by it (Van de Castle, 1994).

Jerome, born to a wealthy Christian family in the fourth century, had a dream in which he was uncertain whether he was really a Christian because while he claimed to be Christian, he still admired the teachings of some pagan writers. In the dream he promised never to "deny" God again by reading pagan literature.

Jerome became a Bible scholar and consultant and when called to Rome in 382 to translate the Bible from Hebrew into Latin, the official language of the Roman Empire, he apparently deliberately mistranslated the Hebrew word for witchcraft, "anan" which was considered a pagan practice, as "observo somnia" which means "observing dreams." Thus, for centuries after, Christian belief and practice regarding dreams was altered. It has only been within the last half of the 20th century that some Christian scholars have begun to approve of the use of dreams as sources of personal information.

Some, like John A. Sanford, an Episcopal priest, now consider dreams as "God's Forgotten Language," a subject he covers in his book by the same name (Sanford, 1968.)

Roy M. Mendelson, M.D., a psychiatrist in private practice in St. Louis, Mo, in his book "The Manifest Dream and Its Use in Therapy," writes about the importance of dream analysis in therapy as a tool to enlighten unconscious processes, which can't be expressed directly. However, he recognizes that each dreamer employs a preferred set of symbols and translation of the symbols and without knowing the dreamer, interpreting the dream can result in an error in the translation (Mendelson, 1990).

Working with your own dreams, you are already working with an expert, since nobody knows better what a symbol represents to you than you. And if you're not quite sure what it means, it's back to the old "balloon method" described earlier on page 14.

Dreams are especially valuable in working with children. You may have noticed that as an adult you don't dream as much as you did when you were a child. That may actually seem like a good thing if you were one of those unfortunate kids who had nightmares (which possibly reflect memories carried over from past lives). Up until about age 3, children often verbalize events from past lives, which they remember but usually the adults in their world pass them off as an overactive imagination. Referring to "when I was big" is a common statement usually squelched by grown-ups eager to correct the child that he was never "big" but he will be big someday when he grows up. I know. I did it myself with my grandchildren before I learned all this stuff. These memories also may surface in dreams or nightmares.

To this day I could kick myself when I think of the time my three-year-old grandson was going "plinking" (target practicing) with his dad and grandfather. I said, "This will be the first time you've shot a gun."

My grandson replied, "No grandma. I shot a gun before when I was big." And he proceeded to show me how he had carried a gun at his shoulder, demonstrating how he marched, like soldier.

How I wish I knew then what I know now.

Even nightmares can be a positive thing when you understand how to work with the symbols. By working with dreams, the dreamer can identify the "monster" pursuing him in sleep time. Once that "monster" is identified (perhaps an abusive parent, a bullying playmate or a demanding teacher), the nightmares usually stop. Sometimes, professional help is needed, as in the case of the abusive parent, since there isn't much a child or anyone else can do to change the behavior of an adult other than change his or her response to it. And in some cases where the behavior may be life threatening, a child will need professional intervention and help. Simply figuring out the "monster" in his/her dreamtime isn't going to solve the problem. However, it's a start, which is why many therapists today will ask clients, both children and adults, about their dreams.

G. William Domhoff, professor of psychology and sociology at the University of California in Santa Cruz, has done extensive work on "Finding Meaning in Dreams: A Quantitative Approach," with studies of dreams, dream series and dream sets, using a system developed by Calvin S. Hall and Robert Van de Castle.

Dream series are dream reports from a certain type of person, e.g. men, women, children, Americans, schizophrenics, etc. Dream sets are certain types of dreams such as falling, flying, appearing naked in public, etc. The Domhoff and Hall-Van de Castle work provided some great background material for my own study on dreams, listing a systematic, scientific method of content analysis in 10 general categories. They are:

1. Characters
2. Social interactions
3. Activities
4. Striving: Success and failure
5. Misfortunes and good fortunes
6. Emotions
7. Physical surroundings: Settings and objects
8. Descriptive elements
9. Food and eating
10. Elements from the past.

Each category is important when working with dreams in general and especially when working with dreams to solve physical and emotional problems, because they provide a way of breaking down the dream content into parts. Then the client (in this case, yourself) can separate what the elements mean and come up with a picture of what the combined elements indicate.

Sometimes medications affect dreams. As the dreamer, you will know if your dreams have changed since you began taking a medication. This, however, does not mean you can't work with your dreams if you are on some type of medication. It's just something to be aware of that may change the dream content. For example, the colors in a dream may be more vivid when taking medication. But that doesn't mean you can't figure them out.

Margaret, one of the women in my study, said she did not dream at all once she began taking medicine/treatment for liver cancer. However, after making an effort to remember her dreams, by programming herself to remember them before going to sleep (repeating the seven-syllable command three times – a dream will bring the answer), she was able to obtain information.

Margaret didn't like cats and in one of her dreams, she went into the pantry in her kitchen and found cats and kittens resting on all of the shelves. One of the cats was a very large feline that she felt was more threatening than the others.

On her next visit she learned her liver was full of tumors but there was one especially large one the doctors were more concerned about.

Another of Margaret's dreams included different symbols but the same general message. She was home alone when a bunch of strangers began invading her house and "taking over." She described the characters as "unkempt, hippie types" and they just took over her house.

The unwanted visitors, in this dream, were also symbols of the tumors that were "taking over her house" - her body. (Remember – a house or a vehicle usually symbolizes the body.)

But even a scary dream like this can be helpful. The dreamer can program herself to get rid of the unwanted invaders. For example, Margaret might have programmed her dreams so she would shoo the cats (and the "unkempt hippies") out of her house. Perhaps she could have asked for a fierce attack dog to help her with this.

Unfortunately, in this case, Margaret's cancer was too far advanced and she did not survive, but she valued the insight her dreams provided and I will be forever grateful to this courageous woman for the help she provided me with my studies in spite of the fact that she was so very sick at the time.

In any situation where a dreamer is experiencing unwanted "stuff" in his/her house or vehicle, he/she will do well to program dreams immediately to get rid of it, even if initially he/she doesn't have a clue as to what the unwanted "stuff" – be it cats or unkempt hippies or whatever – might represent.

Ask for a dream in which your dog chases the invaders away. Borrow a dream mongoose from the local zoo to get rid of the snakes (if you're seeing snakes in your house in your dreams and you're uncomfortable with snakes). Imagination is the key. And if you aren't sure what to do to get rid of whatever type of creature is invading your house in your dreams, visit the library and read up on the life cycle and habits of that particular creature and what its natural enemies are. Then ask for one of those natural enemies to show up in your dreams and get rid of the unpleasant critters.

I'm sure you've heard the expression, "A picture is worth a thousand words." I'd like to paraphrase that a bit to say, "An example is worth a thousand words."

The following examples from the dream studies I did while writing my dissertation, and in the years that followed, will give you an idea of what to look for in dreams and what they might be telling you. The names of all these folks, of course, have been changed to protect their privacy.

Shortly before Angela's husband, Don, was diagnosed with pancreatic cancer, Angela dreamed of losing her wallet (losing her security, which, in this case turned out to represent both financial and emotional). She and Don were walking along a snowy trail near their home. In the dream they get to the end of the trail (probably representing the end of Don's life) by a courthouse and she realizes she has lost her wallet and has to go back and look for it. Don says he'll wait while she looks. (This, again, was very unlike her husband. In real life he would have helped her, but now she was on her own.) She is heading back down the trail when the dream ends.

"At this point in time, Don was very sick but we had not yet received a diagnosis," Angela said. "I knew, from the content of the dream, that an end to something was coming up and that I was worried about my financial security. Looking back, I think the courthouse symbolized the legal things I was going to have to deal with after his death."

In this case, there wasn't anything Angela or Don could do to prevent the inevitable. However, this dream, and others that were similar, prompted Don to sign over his retirement package to Angela after he was diagnosed with pancreatic cancer, so that Angela would not lose her financial security upon his death. That made it possible for Angela to continue working from home as a graphic artist rather than having to go out and look for a job.

Donna's dream didn't involve symbols at all, but was very direct. Donna, 35, was a devoted exerciser. As a child she had enjoyed working on a trapeze. One day she discovered the manager of the gym had added a set of rings, suspended from the ceiling to the equipment. She didn't have time to try them out after her aerobics class that day, but she was anxious to get back the next morning and see if she could still do some of the acrobatics she remembered from her childhood work on the trapeze on the rings. That night she dreamed that the rope on one of the rings had broken.

Imagine her shock when she went to the gym the next day, all set to try the rings, and discovered that the rope on one of the rings had broken and another client at the gym was injured as a result.

Anne, a 50-year-old office manager who previously lived in Wisconsin, had several physical and emotional problems, which presented themselves in her dreams. Among them were marital stress, asthma, chronic constipation, allergies and sciatica.

On October 14, 2001, Anne was living in Montana, but she dreams she is in her former office in Wisconsin (a place she doesn't like). Everyone in the office is taking a rest (something she knows she needs, but isn't able to do). She has to go to the bathroom (a necessity, probably referring to the needed rest and the need to eliminate some things from her life). She can't find a toilet; only an empty can, so she uses the can and dumps it in the toilet that wasn't there before. (Using the can indicates finding a way to accomplish the necessary.)

At this point in her life Anne, a non-traditional student, was completing an associates degree and considering further education. Her health was poor, which was one of the reasons she wasn't getting enough rest. Between working full time and going to school she needed rest. Using the can and then dumping it in the toilet that suddenly appeared AFTER using the can indicated she would find a way to do whatever was necessary to complete her goals.

In another of Anne's dreams, five years later, in October 2006, she is in her childhood home in Wisconsin (indicating a problem that goes back a long way, probably to childhood) and an aunt and uncle come to visit. Her house is very dirty. She serves dessert, but while doing this, she changes two baby diapers at the table. There is a pot of yeast fermenting in the kitchen. She describes the dirty diapers and yeast as "gross" and the furniture as being "all over the place" and she wants to throw the old furniture out.

The dirty house indicates "dirty" body, probably referring to her constipation and sinusitis. The pot of yeast symbolizes her head and infected sinuses, possibly caused by a fungus infection. Dessert would indicate something desirable. Changing the diapers indicated wanting to make a change. Furniture "all over" indicated scattered thoughts and a need to toss out old thoughts/things.

A third dream from Anne's journal is this one from March 2007.

She has a pet beaver and it is very loving. (In waking life she is allergic to all animals.) So we looked up "beaver" in "A Dictionary of Dreams" by Gustavus Hindman Miller. Traditional symbols sometimes don't mean anything to the individual, but in this case it did. A dream of beavers was said to foretell the dreamer would obtain comfortable circumstances by patient striving. Anne accepted this as an explanation since she was still patiently striving for an education, by that time, towards a master's degree. The fact that she was not allergic to the beaver in her dreams indicated a need to have something or someone in her life that she could tolerate – someone who would not be judgmental.

The beaver (generally associated with busyness) was probably also a symbol of her busy life.

Barbara, a married woman, age 58, was working as a hairstylist at the time of this dream. She was tired of her work as a hairstylist in a nursing home and was worried about her son being out of work.

No novice at working with dreams, Barbara frequently relied on them as messages from God to solve her problems. She considered the following dreams to be God's response to her problems.

In the first dream, in 1995 (month unknown) she hears a dream voice, which she knows to be God, telling her to build a home and offer assisted living to four elderly people. Since she lives in a remote area, she is concerned about who would come there, but the Lord tells her to "build it and they will come" – as in the movie, "Field of Dreams." In the dream she and her husband build the house. They have a lot of problems getting supplies, etc., but the problems always work out.

So in real life, she and her husband build the "dream house." It takes 2½ years, but the house is finally finished, she quits her job as a hairstylist and opens a home caring for four elderly people.

In another dream, when her son was out of work, she asked for help from God and again, He complied. In the dream, her son goes to work as manager of a radio station.

"The Lord even told me how much money he would make," Barbara said. "When my son called me (in waking life) to meet him for lunch he was excited about finding a job as the manager of a radio station and the salary was just what I'd been told in the dream!"

Neither of these dreams requires analysis. They are two of those rare dreams in which the answer is direct and requires no figuring out. What they do show is the more open and accepting you are of dream messages, the more likely you are to have revelations in your dreams.

Carole programmed her dreams to find an answer to her sinus problem. The answer didn't come immediately but after a few tries, Carole, in her dream, is in a health food store where she used to work. A local doctor and the man who owned the store are there (both figures from whom she would feel comfortable accepting advice about a health). A man who is known for being a troublemaker around town comes in and wants to rent the building, but insists he needs the whole building and wants to be sure he also gets the upstairs.

The owner of the store tells Carole she should try seawater.

Working on this dream, we determined that the health food store represented not only a physical body but also the answer to the health question. She was to look for the answer in alternative health (the health food store) rather than seeking a traditional medical solution.

The presence of two male figures with authority in health fields (representing Carole's conscious self) indicated she already had the answer. She may just not have thought of it yet on the waking level. The fact that the two male figures are the owner of the health food store and a doctor indicated the answer she was receiving to this question about health could be trusted.

The man wanting the "whole building including the upstairs" indicated a need to take care of her "whole self." The upstairs (representing the sinuses) was especially important. The suggestion of salt water prompted Carole to look in her natural medicine books where she found a reference to using a simple saline solution made of salt and distilled water to help clear up a sinus condition.

The method called for a half pint of distilled or boiled and cooled water, ¼ teaspoon salt and ¼ teaspoon baking soda. A 10 or 12 cc syringe (minus the needle) which can be purchased at the drug store, is then used to squirt saline into the nose, twice in each side, one side at a time, while holding the other nostril shut.

"It really made me gag in the beginning but it has worked great for clearing my nose, especially in the morning," Carole said.

A Neti pot, one of those things that looks like an Aladdin's lamp, was another suggestion.

This dream is a perfect example of advice, in a dream, coming from a person one would trust and rely on for that type of information and therefore, the dreamer is more likely to accept it. Carole's dream advice came from a health food storeowner in the presence of a physician. Had this advice come from a painter, for example, Carole might not have so readily accepted the answer as valid.

Sometimes dreams/nightmares can be very frightening. They might even cause you to doubt your sanity, but when you are willing to devote the effort to dissecting dreams they often turn out to be "common sense."

I'll share these dreams from Elizabeth because they are the kind of dreams a person is almost embarrassed to talk about. I'm grateful to Elizabeth for sharing it.

In one dream, monsters that are going to eat her are pursuing Elizabeth. Instead, they kill a teenage boy and make her eat his body.

Elizabeth, a young mother who was under a lot of emotional stress, was very upset by this one, especially since she had previously had two dreams about cannibalism involving her young son, which were very disturbing.

Cannibalism is usually an indication of depriving part of oneself to strengthen another part or living off the energy of others instead of generating your own creative energy. It can also indicate a desire to take someone or something "within" to protect it.

Elizabeth felt these interpretations made sense. Her son had just started school and was busy with activities that took him away from her and home. She was worried about his safety (wanting to devour him to protect him). Since she was so busy with her family, she was neglecting her own creative energy, which was indicated by living off the energy of another person – eating the teenage boy. (A teenage boy would have a lot of energy.)

This explanation put her mind at ease because the thought of cannibalism was repulsive and frightening. But the dream had nothing to do with actual cannibalism. It had to do with protecting her child and denying her own creativity.

Now wasn't that a relief?

CHAPTER THIRTEEN

Dreams and superstitions – our subconscious guides

During my Catholic school years in the 1940s and 50s, anything having to do with the unexplained was taboo. There were many times I got in trouble for asking questions about such things. Dreams and superstitions were among them. But as I grew older, and wiser, I began to see a pattern in the messages we get from dreams and from superstitions as well. When you think about it, superstitions all began with a reason. Perhaps the man who walked under a ladder got a bucket of paint dropped on his head. So walking under a ladder became unlucky when actually the superstition was a safety precaution.

It reminds me of the story of a woman who always cut both ends off a roast until she was asked why. Not knowing why, she asked her mother. Her mother didn't know why so she asked her grandmother. Turns out the grandmother's roasting pan was too small for most of the roasts for her large family so she sliced off the ends to make it fit and three generations followed suit without ever knowing why. It was a "good" reason in the beginning but it no longer applied.

Armando Benitez, author of "Sheer Superstition – Outmaneuvering Fate" (Hampton Roads Publishing Co. Inc., 2000) alludes to the value of superstition and dreams in solving physical and emotional and sometimes even financial problems.

A frequenter of horse races in his earlier days, Benitez tells how overheard comments and seemingly casual observances prompted him to bet on certain horses that resulted in wins. What does this have to do with dreams? A lot. Learning to closely observe the content in a dream can have the same effect on problem solving as paying attention to the subtle signs from the universe before betting on a horse. The symbols are your subconscious mind's way of attracting your attention.

Superstitions, like dreams, boil down to learning the art of a subconscious divination of the future, whether that be betting on a horse or acting on a warning about an infected gall bladder.

The dream mentioned earlier of the young woman who was perplexed as to the meaning of the "businesses" on the highway and the relationship they had to her bothersome dream of seeing her children sinking in murky water is another example of symbols and a play on words. The "businesses" in the dream were indicative of the "busyness" in her life.

When working with dreams always look at other seemingly unrelated meanings for the same word that may provide a clue to the answer to your problem. A knotted rope may mean something that is "not" in your thinking, indicating you have not enough or are not able or not allowed to do something. A cat in a dream might indicate a concern over "catty" behavior. Dreams help us see the truth about ourselves so don't be too quick to dismiss "cattiness" as someone else's problem when it is affecting you. It may be that your own cattiness is causing an emotional/relationship problem in your life. This is especially true if you are very upset about the cattiness. It reminds me of a line from Shakespeare – methinks the lady protests too much. Remember, every one and every thing in a dream, usually, is an aspect of yourself. So if your mate or friend, in a dream is being catty, or you see a cat in a dream, look in the mirror and be willing to question yourself. It may solve your relationship problem.

Loosing teeth is a common symbol in a dream. It could indicate the need for a trip to the dentist but it could also mean you are losing control of something and feel powerless. It could also indicate something as unmysterious as concern about your dentist appointment next week.

Losing hair is another one that could indicate a physical problem but it could also indicate forgetfulness, or lacking strength to deal with a problem.

Look at every possible play on words you can think of that a dream symbol might hold, and chances are you'll get the message. Granted it takes a little practice but like everything else, dream analysis tends to get better with practice.

In writing on dreams in "Sheer Superstition," Armando Benitez shares some valuable information aside from what to look for in betting on a horse race. The following is from Chapter 22 – Spinning the Thirty-Million Dollar Dream: (My comments in brackets.)

"Sometimes we make our intrusions into the arcane in a conscious manner, as when we consult a fortuneteller or peer into a crystal ball. And sometimes we do it involuntarily such as when we have prophetic dreams.

"Even long before Joseph and the pharaoh of Egypt, dreams have always been the most obvious way of divining the future. But besides their prophetic content dreams can carry a wealth of information of a more prosaic nature. In "The Art of Creation" Arthur Koestler told of how the solution to a vexing problem in chemistry came to a famed scientist in a dream after he had all but given up trying to solve it. Possibly, a visionary dreamer among our remote cave dwelling ancestors was first guided into making fire by a dream.

"We can therefore expect to extract both types of information from our dreams; prophetic visions of things to come and practical solutions to problems in the present. A common error in the interpretation of dreams is trying to interpret them by attaching set formulas to situations and objects in them, as the ancients did. The applicable meanings will differ vastly from one individual to another. And more often than not the meaning is impossible to decipher until after the event announced by the dream has occurred.

"Warnings of impending unfavorable events (or conditions) can often be intuitively divined even if the specific event remains a puzzle. Such as the dream of Polycrates' daughter, as told by Herodotus. In a dream she saw her father suspended in the air, washed by Zeus and anointed by the sun. Deeply disturbed, she tried to dissuade her father from heeding the summons of the Persian Oroetes, who had requested his presence in Sardis. But Polycrates ignored the warning and went anyway, only to be crucified by the treacherous Oroetes who left him out in the rain and the sun to die – to be "washed" by Zeus and "anointed" by the sun."

In most dream books, Benitez says, nearly every dream, with a monotonous regularity, seems to herald either trouble or an end to trouble. But life is nothing but one long problem, he says, therefore a dream announcing problems seems redundant. Additionally, Benitez says, most of the dream meanings, originating as they did thousands of years ago, have long since ceased to hold the same meaning. [Again, what a symbol means to YOU is what is important. And obviously dream symbols from ancient times aren't going to include a cell phone or a microwave oven. So what you need to look at is what they mean to you. A cell phone – communication, cellular memory, etc. A microwave oven – heating, altering of nutrients, etc.]

Revelatory dreams, Benitez says, can be of two different types. They can be visions of things as yet nonexistent; visions of the future and the information can come in a completely disguised shape, more often than not defying interpretation. Or they can transmit physically existing information, which would normally be hidden from the dreamer, and indeed, hidden from all human knowledge.

We should not try to interpret our dreams into explicit language, or scrutinize them too closely for hidden meanings, Benitez writes. We should only let our dreams serve as a subconscious impulse that will incline us towards a course of action in our everyday affairs. Additionally, when we struggle too openly to decipher the meaning of a dream, the guardians of the arcane (according to Benitez) find the means to further confound us by providing us with an erroneous interpretation.

As with any type of "divination," be it palmistry, fortune telling, or crystal ball reading, the important thing is to not let it become an obsession. If you have a gut feeling a dream is warning you of an impending health problem, see your doctor. But don't allow dream analysis to become a kind of hypochondriacal diagnostic activity.)

CHAPTER FOURTEEN

Getting off the Ground

Of all the dreams I have worked with - and there have been hundreds of them, my own and others included - this is probably the one that stands out the most in terms of the dream world reflecting the awakened state. It's a dream my friend, Darlene, a writer, experienced.

Darlene has enjoyed dreams of flying since she was a child, so much so that she actually looked forward to going to bed, which is pretty unusual for a kid. She even wrote a children's book, "Flying Dreams," published by Mothers House Publishing in 2008.

Unfortunately, for the past few years, Darlene has been on medication, which has caused a considerable weight gain, and she is no longer able to fly in her dreams.

"I'm so heavy I can't get off the ground," she says.

Her dreams are reflecting the condition of her physical body.

Darlene is working on the weight problem which is especially difficult, given that it's the medication causing the weight gain and not just a case of eating too much. She is determined to fly in her dreams once more, and not, as she so humorously puts it, as the Goodyear Blimp!

Many experts in the field of dream analysis feel it is better to NOT know a person's background or anything about them when analyzing a dream. That way there are no preconceived notions. My feeling is that it helps to know something about the person simply because it eliminates a lot of guesswork. But there again, we're back to that old "gut feeling." I have successfully done dream analysis online without knowing a thing about the person. It has worked because the person on the computer at the other end either experiences that "got it!" feeling or an uncertain feeling that this just isn't quite right.

For example, water is a pretty much universal symbol of an emotional condition, so notice if your water is flowing smoothly, crashing on the rocks, muddy, or maybe even has a reflection in it. The reflection could be something you are (or should be) reflecting on.

Work with symbology until you hit the nail on the head, but don't struggle with it. Of course, in working with your own dreams you already know your own background, wants, desires, health issues, etc. What you don't have is the subconscious information to help you with those problems and that is the stuff dreams are made of.

Darlene's weight gain transferred to her dream world and she can no longer fly in her dreams and enjoy the nighttime adventures she loved, but I have no doubt once she loses some of the weight (and her dreams may very well provide information to help with that), she will be soaring above the treetops once again.

You have probably noticed that most dreams take you back to childhood and people, places and things from long ago. There are different schools of thought as to why this happens; but in general, dreams are set in the past because they include people, thoughts, buildings and situations you experienced in your formative years and therefore they are most likely to be ingrained in your psyche.

For example, a "teaching" dream that is trying to provide you with information is more likely to take place in the elementary school you attended while growing up than in the college you attended in later years. This is especially true if you enjoyed elementary or high school and have pleasant memories of that place. You are more likely to accept information coming from that place because it is one you trust. Not that you didn't trust college and your professors. It's just that elementary school came first. Hence dreams often include being unable to find your way to your next class in high school, being unable to get your locker open, walking down the hall naked, etc. Being unable to find your way would indicate uncertainty about where to go in your waking life. Being unable to open that locker probably means you are trying to solve the problem and haven't found the right combination in the form of an answer, and walking naked down the halls would indicate you feel vulnerable about some situation and possibly you are concerned about being exposed.

I used to dream a lot, and occasionally still do, about being in high school, losing my class schedule and not knowing where to go – an indication of being puzzled in life about something and not knowing which way to turn. Asking for a dream in which I found the principal's office and asked for a new schedule stopped the dream. That resolution may have spilled over into real life, resolving something I was anxious about, even though, at the time, I was not aware of being anxious about anything.

Many lifelong problems originate in childhood and kids don't always grow up in "Leave It To Beaver" homes. A dream that takes you into the past may be pointing out where a problem began. A dream of your mother telling you girls can't be doctors or radio announcers or boys can't be nurses may be showing you where your doubts about your profession began, even though you love your work and are good at it. It may also explain where your doubts about going into a "nontraditional" occupation are coming from.

This dream from Tess illustrates how opinions formed in childhood can affect a person for the rest of their lives – or at least until they realize that type of thinking is no longer valid.

Tess dreamed she was in the attic of her parents' house, only this time she entered it in some new way. She is amazed at all the new stuff she finds and then realizes it was stuff she already knew was there. She's just seeing it from a different angle. She realizes she must clean the attic because she is moving and needs to take the new stuff with her.

In her waking life, Tessa has never considered herself to be very smart. In grade school she excelled in creative things like art and writing, but had extreme difficulty with math and science. Consequently she saw herself as "dumb" because creativity was seen as not being as important as logical, scientifically based, reasoning.

In addition to forming her own negative opinion about herself, her impression of herself as being "dumb" was reinforced by teachers who gave her poor grades and her father, who was excellent in math and became extremely frustrated with his young daughter who just didn't seem to "get it."

Because Tess considered herself to be "stupid" she didn't even consider going on to college in spite of her talent in art and writing. Thankfully a high school teacher recognized her potential and recommended her for a scholarship. To Tess's surprise, she maintained a 3.5 grade point average throughout college. The only thing that brought her average down was the dreaded math, so she took only what was absolutely required in that field and actually enjoyed her studies.

Going back to her parents' attic, in the dream, indicated the head/brain area of her body. (Remember – a house is usually a symbol of the dreamer's body or state of consciousness.) Tess has always seen herself as "stupid" but in this dream she enters the attic (the brain) from a new angle (she did not recall how she got there – only that it wasn't in the traditional way of climbing up the stairs) and realizes there is a lot of stuff (intelligence) in the attic that she hadn't noticed before. Now, she realizes it was there all along and she intends to "take it with her" as she moves on in her life.

After some 25 years of considering herself "stupid," Tess's dream enabled her to leave that erroneous perception from her childhood in the past. The dream told her she was intelligent all along – since back when she was living in her parents' house! She just was not aware of her own intelligence because of the negative impression of herself that was reinforced by some of her teachers and others, like her father, who tried to help but were unable to go get through to her in an area where she did not excel (math). (During her college years, she learned she was actually learning disabled in math.)

Dreams of the past, then, apply to present day problems, which may have originated in the past, or they may present information through trusted images from the past with which the dreamer feels comfortable.

Dreams of the past, in which characters are dressed in clothing from another time, before the dreamer's birth, may be past life dreams, which could be the subject of a whole "nother" book. But this doesn't mean that type of dream isn't valid. Present day problems, physical and emotional, are often carried over from other lifetimes, just like physical characteristics and mannerisms can be picked up from an ancestor. Sometimes past lives are actually genetic memory – a memory passed on through the genes of an ancestor. So dreams in which you and the other characters are dressed "in costume" may carry an equally valid message about something happening in your life today that began before this lifetime.

Moira, a teller at a bank, was often frustrated because people wouldn't pay attention to her ideas. In a series of repetitive dreams, Moira saw herself in some type of tribal culture where she kept trying to warn her people that they were about to be attacked. No one would listen because she was a woman.

Once we figured out the dreams and that "being a woman" in 2005 no longer made her information unimportant, she developed more confidence in presenting her ideas and almost magically, people began to listen.

Sometimes, of course, we do dream of being dressed in costume or being at a party where everyone is in costume. The key to understanding if this dream is a dream from a past life is to be aware of EVERYTHING in the dream. If everything is in an old-fashioned context, for example, everyone is wearing long dresses, traveling by horse and buggy, the buildings are all in the style of another era, then it is most likely a past life dream.

On the other hand, if the dreamer is wearing an old-fashioned dress and traveling in a 2011 Lexus, the dream is telling the dreamer her attitudes and ideas are old-fashioned and she needs to come into the 21st century.

Costumes in an otherwise "modern" dream may also indicate the roles you play. If you are a doctor in your dream and you aren't a doctor in real life, your dream may be telling you that you have the potential of being a healer of some kind. If you are a teacher in a dream, that dream may be saying you have information you need to share with others. Are you dressed as a police officer? Maybe you are being too controlling or authoritative. Or maybe you need to become more in charge. The meaning, as always, depends on the dreamer and what is going on in his/her life.

A fairly common dream in my experience as a dream analyst is a dream of being killed or harmed by a spouse or significant other when the dreamer is, in reality, experiencing problems in a relationship.

Most often this indicates that the dreamer him/herself is killing or harming him/herself by remaining in this relationship, at least in the way the relationship is going at the present time. I have never seen it be a warning that the other person was about to actually kill or harm the dreamer. Rather, the dreamer is killing or harming him/herself by the way he/she is responding in the relationship. The dreamer may need to get out of the relationship or if that isn't a desired option, change his/her present situation by responding differently to the actions of the significant other. If being in a relationship is "killing you," even symbolically, you need to take a serious look at whether it's worth maintaining that relationship, whether it's personal, romantic or business.

Sometimes symbols in dreams may appear overly large or small when compared to real life. Large symbols, like a huge plate of food, may indicate you are eating too much. A tiny amount of food or tiny items of food may indicate a need for more self-nurturing and that nurturing can take the form of actual food or it may simply mean nurturing in the form of allowing yourself to enjoy life more. Use your imagination. Notice what is out of balance in a dream. Exaggerated size, large or small, is calling your attention to something that is in excess or deficient in your life.

Sometimes sketching a dream symbol is of more help than writing about it, especially if you are artistically inclined. Just as you would write down your dream immediately upon awakening, make a quick sketch of the dream symbol and then fill in later with colors or details. For those who are more artistically inclined, keeping a box of crayons near the recorder and/or notepad used for journaling dreams is a good idea. A quick sketch will anchor the memory for you.

Colors are important since they often indicate how the dreamer feels about a symbol. If the plants in your dream garden are gray, you're probably not feeling well in your awake life. Program your dreams to change the color of your plants and it will transfer into your waking life. A good example of this is my pumpkin dream mentioned in the beginning of this book. In my pumpkin dream, when I was very sick in my waking life, my plants and fruit were withered and dying on the vine but after struggling to climb to the top of the hill, I could see the other side and there were acres and acres of beautiful pumpkins which told me my health would improve. I just had to work at it (struggle uphill). In that dream, my pumpkins and vines were brown and dull on the hilly side, but became vibrant green and orange on the other side.

Dreams can provide messages to help us deal with grief, depression and emotional problems.

Audrey Carli, in "When Jesus Holds Our Hand" (Carli, 1987) writes about the death of her husband, Dave, in 1983 and the answers she received in dreams to the emotional problems surrounding her tragic loss. One of the dreams was a message from God, telling her to "turn your grief into energy for the glory of God." This dream prompted her to resume her career as a freelance writer. She has since developed a writing and speaking ministry, helping others deal with grief.

Like so many things, dream work can be more fun when it's shared. In the beginning, especially, you may benefit from forming a dream group or at least finding a friend with whom you can discuss your dreams and what the symbols mean to you. Often people who are close to you will pick up on the meaning of a symbol you are puzzled about, simply because you're too close to see it yourself. You know that old expression about not being able to see the forest for the trees? We are so closely involved with our own problems and our own perceptions about them that it's easy to miss something that may be very obvious to someone else. And a word to the wise – if you adamantly disagree with someone else's observation, be willing to explore it a little more. Sometimes the things we deny the most are exactly where the answer to our problem lies.

Sometimes you'll luck out and a single dream will provide the answer in a fairly direct way, like Audrey Carli's dream about turning her grief into energy for the glory of God. But more often than not, it's going to involve some work to decipher these cryptic messages revealed by our subconscious and higher self in dreams.

Subconscious messages come from information buried in the past, like a fear of water that goes back to when you slipped underwater in your baby bathtub and aren't consciously aware of it. Messages from your higher self come from the super conscious part of you – the part that knows the answers and is willing to share the information with a little persuasion. So ask yourself before you go to bed for a dream that will answer your concerns about your fear of water. Once you have the answer, more than likely, the problem will be solved. If you fear going through a traumatic experience ask to be an observer in your dream rather than a participant. Remember to repeat it three times before going to sleep and remember the seven-syllable command – something like "I see why I fear wa-ter."

After jotting down your initial dream immediately upon awakening, take time to separate the symbols to see what emerges. Don't look for a story line because often there isn't one. It's just a message – not a story. And the message may be something as simple as you aren't "in the drivers seat" in terms of your life. Someone else is directing where you go and how you do it. This might be indicated in a dream or a series of dreams in which you are a passenger in a vehicle rather than the driver.

Next, give the dream a title and a date, and finally write out the symbols like a spelling list, down the left side of the page.

Here's a sample dream to illustrate what I mean.

Barbara, the mother of two adult daughters had this dream.

Her daughters are visiting and they are outdoors near a basement entry area. There are bells on ropes from a Christmas play and tomatoes are hanging on the ropes. One daughter discovers the tomatoes are rotten and they leave.

Next Barbara sees a helicopter in the distance and realizes one of her daughters is flying it and the other is hanging out the bottom. She thinks, "Oh, my God, she forgot to buckle up!" The helicopter lands and the daughter piloting the helicopter says she lost the other one. Barbara then hears her lost daughter crying and sees her walking, but the daughter is bruised on her right side. She thinks the problem isn't too bad, but then realizes her daughter's top right femur is open and bent up, like a chicken wing.

Next we list the symbols down the left side of the page and directly across from the symbols, list what they mean to you – the dreamer.

Daughters – children (as in brain children or ambitions) Also possibly her younger self.

Outdoors – outside of yourself

Basement entry – access to the subconscious

Bells – a sound to alert you to something

Christmas play – something out of sync (since the dream setting was in the summer)

Rotten tomatoes – nurturing food but it is spoiled

Helicopter – rising above a situation

Pilot (daughter) – A creative part of the self in charge of rising above the situation.

Other daughter hanging from chopper – part of the self in a perilous position

Injuries – something wrong in the right thigh area of the dreamer's body

Looking at the meanings of these symbols to the dreamer, it becomes obvious Barbara has a problem that originated outside her (she is outside the house) but her subconscious has access to that information (the basement entry).

Her subconscious is trying to get her attention (the bells) that something is out of sync in her life (the tomatoes and Christmas decorations).

The tomatoes, being red, may indicate inflammation. This is something Barbara suspected.

Her daughters, being her children, represent creative aspects of herself (brain children) or possibly her "younger" self - something that happened when she was younger.

The helicopter piloted by one of the daughters indicates the dreamer is rising above the problem, looking for the proper perspective on it.

The injuries indicate something was going on in Barbara's body in her upper right thigh. At the time we worked with the dream it was not apparent but a few weeks later, she reported having an attack of sciatica in her right leg. It was at that point she determined the red, rotten tomatoes might have been a warning of inflammation.

No, it's not "simple" to work with dreams. It takes time and effort, but it is also fascinating and informative and especially useful when your health care practitioner insists there is "nothing wrong."

Working with your dreams, more often than not, you can come up with an answer on your own. Once you have your dream diagnosis, you may want to let your health care practitioner know about it (and hope he/she is open to listening). If not, you might want to find a health care person who is.

You can also program your dreams for an answer. Each night before going to bed, think about your problem and tell yourself, at least three times – a dream will bring the answer. (Or a similar seven-syllable command.) You might want to be more specific and say something like "dreams tell me why my nose bleeds."

In the dream studies I did for my doctoral dissertation, I used a dream or series of dreams collected from 14 people, ranging in age from children to senior citizens. Of those 14 dreamers, 100% of the dreams of 12 of them indicated physical and emotional concerns. Of the 176 dreams of one of the women, 159 (90%) indicted physical and emotional concerns and with the remaining subject who shared 8 dreams, 6 (75%) showed physical and emotional concerns.

With a percentage like that, if I had any doubts before doing my study about the validity of dreams and their relationship to waking life, they were all dispelled.

Psychotherapy is expensive and the general purpose is to bring the client to a realization of his/her own problems. By learning to spot clues in your dreams, you can counsel yourself. There's nothing wrong with getting professional help as well. In fact, it's a good idea, but by paying close attention to your dreams you have the advantage of your own inner counselor – your higher self, providing the answers or at least clues for you to work with. By keeping a journal of your dreams, over time you can monitor changes that occur in your waking life.

Books on traditional dream symbols can be helpful, but in the long run your own perceptions and realization of what the symbols mean specifically to you – not the general populace - will give you the answers you need. By becoming aware of the messages relayed in our dreams, it's possible to detect pathological and emotional situations even before they manifest and to monitor them when they do become apparent, thus giving you a "heads up" in dealing with the situation. This, alone, is very empowering. By programming your dreams to obtain more positive outcomes and images, you can actually do something about your problem, be it physical or emotional, rather than just sit back and let it happen.

In the case of physical illness, when your doctor is open to dream interpretation you can assist in your own diagnosis and treatment by discussing your dream with your doctor. Dreams were once relied on as a valuable source of information by some of the most famous physicians in the history of the world, Hippocrates, the Father of Medicine, among them. Modern scientific studies, combined with Christian beliefs that viewed dream analysis as sorcery for many years, put this valuable tool on the back burner, but thankfully dreams are no longer being dismissed as meaningless, nighttime fantasies by much of the traditional medical establishment.

Of course there are potential risks, albeit minor ones, in focusing too much on dreams for answers. Like anything else, dream analysis can be overdone and result in a person becoming fixated on dreams to the point he/she becomes hypochondriachal, looking for a health message in every dream.

It's said there are no "nonsense" dreams. Every dream has meaning, but there are times when the meaning just isn't that important, like the time I dreamed of picking strawberries all night after picking strawberries all day! There was a message there, all right, but it didn't mean much. I had simply spent more time than I should have picking strawberries and I was tired of it. The dream was telling me I had overdone. Nothing mysterious about that. Some dreams, like this one, are just "day residue" dreams, replaying the events of the day.

Others, like Scrooge's dream of Marley's ghost in Charles Dickens "A Christmas Carol," may be, as Scrooge himself said, "…an undigested bit of beef, a blot of mustard, a crumb of cheese, or a fragment of underdone potato. There is more of gravy than grave about you, whatever you are."

It's true; that type of a dream does reflect a physical condition (indigestion) but it isn't necessarily a serious physical problem that the dreamer should be concerned about unless it is repeated over time. However, if you recall, Scrooge's dreams also resolved an emotional issue and he became a better and happier man as a result.

Rather than dwell on each and every dream, the key is to pay attention to those which seem to have unusual content or which repeat themselves. The intensity of feelings about a dream is a good gauge as to whether a dream holds a significant message. If the feeling is intense, that's a good indication the subconscious or higher self is trying to get the dreamer to pay attention.

When seeking answers to physical and emotional concerns, it's important to remember that dreams can be programmed to provide answers. It may take a little work to translate them, just as it would take some effort to translate a letter from a friend who is writing to you in a language you don't understand.

It reminds me of my friend, Marianne, who is German and sometimes sends me "forwards" on the computer in German. At first I had no clue what they were about, but after several years of receiving her German "forwards" I have a pretty good idea, even though I don't understand the language. Familiarity is the key. As you become more familiar with the dream symbols you'll find yourself recognizing things more readily and without putting a lot of effort into figuring them out.

It is my hope that doctors and therapists of the future will accept dream analysis as just another diagnostic and treatment tool. But in the meantime, until they catch up, we can do it ourselves.

REFERENCES

In alphabetical order by author/editor

Amar, Silvana, "The Bedside Dream Dictionary," Skyhorse Publishing, Inc. 2007

Barrett, Deidre, "Trauma and Dreams," Harvard University Press, Cambridge, Mass., London, England, 1996.

Bethard, Betty, "The Dream Book: Symbols for Self Understanding," Inner Light Foundation, Novato, Calif., 1987

Benitez, Armando, "Sheer Superstition – Outmaneuvering Fate," Hampton Roads, 2000

Butler, Gail, "Crystal and Gemstone Divination"

Campbell, Don, "The Mozart Effect," Avon books, 1997

Carli, Audrey, "When Jesus Holds Our Hand," AMC Publishing Co., Stambaugh, Mich. 1987.

Domhoff, William (paper) "Finding Meaning in Dreams: A Quantitative Approach," "The Scientific Study of Dream Content." 1997.

Eason, Cassandra, "The Illustrated Directory of Healing Stones."

Fried, Stephen, "Bitter Pills – Inside the Hazardous World of Legal Drugs," Bantam Books, New York, 1998.

Garfield, Patricia, Ph.D., "Creative Dreaming," Ballantine Books, Edition, 1976 and 1985.

Goldberg, Bruce Dr., "New Age Hypnosis," Llewellyn Publications, 1999

Kasatkin, Vasily, National Enquirer, 1975

Wilmer, H.A., from "Trauma and Dreams," by Deirdre Barrett, Harvard University Press, Cambridge, Mass., London England, 1996 (from Journal of the American Academy of Psychoanalysis, 1982, "Vietnam and Madness: Dreams of Schizophrenic Veterans."

McGarey, Wm. A. M.D., The Edgar Cayce Remedies," Bantam Books, New York, 1983.

Mendelson, Roy M., M.D., "The Manifest Dream and Its Use In Therapy," Jason Aronson, Inc, Northvale, New Jersey, 1990.

Melodie, "Love Is In the Earth Series," Earth – Love Publishing House, Wheatridge, CO 2008

Miller, Gustavus Hindman, "A Dictionary of Dreams," Smithmark Publishers, Inc., New York, 1994.

Raphaell, Katrina, "Crystal Enlightenment – The Transforming Properties of Crystals," and "Healing Stones," Aurora Press, NY 1985

Sabini, Meredith, paper, "Psychother.Psychosom," "Dreams as an Aid in Determining Diagnosis, Prognosis, and Attitude Towards Treatment," 1981.

Sanford, John A., "God's Forgotten Language," Studies from the C.G. Jung Institute, Zurich, Lippencot, Philadelphia and New York, seventh printing, 1968.

Schumann, Walter, "Minerals of the World."

Siegal, Bernie M.D., "Love, Medicine and Miracles," HarperCollins Publishers, 1986.

Tanner, Wilda B. "The Mystical, Magical Marvelous World of Dreams," Sparrow Hawk Press, 1986

Van De Castle, Robert L., Ph.D., "Our Dreaming Mind," Ballantine Books, New York, 1994.

Weiss, Brian, M.D. "Through Time Into Healing," Simon and Schuster, New York, 1992.

Wilmer, H.A., from "Trauma and Dreams," by Deirdre Barrett, Harvard University Press, Cambridge, Mass., London England, 1996 (from Journal of the American Academy of Psychoanalysis, 1982, "Vietnam and Madness: Dreams of Schizophrenic Veterans."

Ziegler, A., "Heart Failure and Aporetic Dreams," 1980.

www.ingramcontent.com/pod-product-compliance
Lightning Source LLC
Chambersburg PA
CBHW031942070426
42450CB00005BA/345